GOING THROUGH HELL TO GET TO HEAVEN

The Harrowing Account of How True Life

Can Turn to True Crime in an Instant

Soyini Taylor Walton

A *Red Carpet DC* Book

Going Through Hell to Get to Heaven

By Soyini Taylor Walton

A *Red Carpet DC* Book

Publishing History:

Red Carpet DC Paperback First Edition / January 2014

For information address:

Red Carpet DC Books

324 Main Street #1608

Laurel, MD 20725

ISBN 978-0-615-94248-3

Available at Amazon.Com, CreateSpace.Com,

SoyiniWalton.Com, and a bookstore near you.

Table of Contents

I dedicate this book to my parents Rae Jean and Jim Taylor. You are more than parents, you are my angels. I love you more than words can say.

So I looked, and behold, a pale horse.
And the name of him who sat on it was
Death, and Hell followed with him.

Revelation 6: 8 a,b (NKJV)

January 14, 2008

I go through my normal Monday morning routine: wake up at 6 a.m., in the gym by 6:30 a.m., out by about 7:15 a.m., go home to shower, and on the road to my job by 8:15 a.m. Depending on traffic, I'm usually in the office around 9 a.m. to take care of some administrative tasks and check in with my district sales manager. By 9:30-ish, I'm out of the office and on my way to my first sales call of the day. I had a great year last year and was one of the company's top sales performers for every quarter of 2007. I plan to do the same in 2008. I have a pretty nice-sized office, but I don't spend too much time there; I really just stop by to pick up or drop off sales proposals. I'm enjoying my corporate job and am making a really good income as a top sales rep.

Every morning at about 9:30 a.m. EST, I call my parents in California to catch up with them as I drive to my first sales visit for the day. Because California is three hours behind, it works out perfectly for me to talk to them at 9:30 a.m. my time. And since I no longer live in Cali with them, this ritual makes me feel like I'm giving them a hug before I leave for work for the day.

It's a good time in my life, and I'm thankful for things the way they are. So many wonderful things have been happening in my life: I bought my first home two and a half years ago; I have a good, stable job and a very comfortable income; and I just recently finished my Life Coach certification program and have started coaching clients on the weekends. Plus, I've been dating a new guy for the past four months, and things are going well with our relationship so far.

I enjoy having downtown Washington, DC as my sales territory. I'm responsible for selling to some of the largest corporations and government agencies in DC, and I usually visit about five accounts per day. I've had some clients as accounts for about two years, so we have become friends. Other clients are new, so I'm building relationships with them. The best part of my job is meeting people as I've always been a very social person. When I was in college, I never dreamed that I would go into sales, but it has turned out to be a really good career move for me because it fits my personality.

As I drive downtown Washington DC, navigating through the traffic, I think about my plans to hang out with friends on the weekend and a list of errands that I need to complete during the week. But, as a very reflective person, I also think about my life and where I want to go next. A very common thought for me is, "Where will my life be one year from now? What will my life look like on January 14, 2009?"

September 2008

I filed for a restraining order today. I can't handle the phone calls anymore, and his constant texting and calling is just too much. His showing up at my door is overwhelming.

I've dated and had many relationships in my life, and I've never had a breakup that was this crazy. It just feels different. When he leaves messages for me, I can hear the desperation in his voice. And there is anger—lots of it. In the beginning, I answered his phone calls, but now he's not making sense, and he won't stop what I consider very aggressive behavior—calling my church, sending me bogus emails, calling friends of mine. He's harassing me. For a few weeks I ignored so much of it, thinking he would just stop, but he doesn't.

I can't concentrate on work because he always interrupts me. Even though I've never seen any signs of violent behavior from him, I just feel something deep down in my spirit that's letting me know things aren't right. My home is supposed to be safe, but now it feels like a prison—I'm afraid to leave it. Whenever I walk outside, I'm careful to look both ways and make sure I don't see him. A few neighbors have told me he's driving a different car now so I won't recognize him.

When you file a restraining order, you have to appear in court in front of a judge. I am so nervous on this Wednesday morning. I haven't seen him in a few weeks, and I don't want to see him. I've never been in a situation like this. I don't like the idea of having to do this, but I need to make it clear to him that his aggressive behavior needs to stop. I don't understand why it's so hard for him to just "leave me alone." As I drive to the courthouse, I'm in disbelief that I'm going to have to see him again. We dated for about a year, and I would've never thought that I'd be in this situation with him.

In my spirit, I know that I'll probably see him as soon as I walk into the building. The hearing is to start at 9:30 a.m., so I deliberately try to arrive as close to that time as possible to avoid having to see him. When I walk into the building, I have to go through a metal detector. As I'm walking through it, I look up to the second floor and I see him. Oh God. I just wish that I didn't have to do this. I know that I have to go up there, but I don't want to. I take a deep breath, and I walk to the escalator. The whole time, I can feel his eyes fixed on my every move. It's amazing that deep down in my spirit, I know his calling and stalking aren't going to stop. The way he's looking at me lets me know that he's going to get his way no matter what.

When I get to the top of the escalator, he starts to talk to me. "I'm so happy to see you. Are you nervous? I'm so nerv-

ous. Baby, we don't have to do this. We can leave right now."
He's speaking as if this is his first experience with a restraining order when in fact this is something that he's very familiar with. I found out later that he has a history of this type of
behavior.

I say nothing to him. I just walk to the bathroom and stay
there for the remaining minutes before the doors of the courtroom open. When I walk out of the bathroom, he's standing
right there. I jump on the inside, but I remain calm on the
outside. I walk into the courtroom, and he walks right next to
me. I am so disgusted to be near him. Something about his
energy seems very aggressive and abusive.

As I walk into the courtroom, I quickly survey the benches
for an empty space. When I find one, I take my seat. The
whole time that I was walking, he was saying something to
me, but I was trying to tune it out. As I sit down, he says,
"I'm going to sit next to you. I miss you so much." And he
plops down right next to me.

I look him dead in his eyes, and I say something like, "Get
away from me. We are in court for a restraining order. Are
you crazy?" He refuses to move, so I say something like,
"I'm going to get up and report you for harassment right now
if you don't get away from me." I get up and move to the other side of the room and sit at the end of the row. I feel so hu-
miliated being in here. When the judge walks into the room, I
just want to scream out, "Get this man away from me!"

I listen to a few cases then I hear my name. I've never ap-
peared before a judge in my life, and I'm terrified. I don't
want to be here at all. I don't even know what this restraining
order will do, but I know that I better start getting things doc-
umented. The judge basically just reviews the paperwork that
I had completed and grants me a restraining order. (In retro-

spect, the restraining order didn't do too much to help me. For me, it was just a piece of paper that did absolutely nothing to prevent the imminent danger awaiting me.) I'm so disgusted standing there in the courtroom that I can't even look over at the "monster." When he speaks to the judge, he puts on his best face. And within five minutes, I'm out of there.

I purposely walk as quickly as I can to get out of there so that I can avoid him. Even though I'm walking briskly, I hear him shout my name a couple of times. I get all the way down the escalator and push open the double doors so that I can get out of the building as quickly as possible. I only make it about 20-25 feet out of the building before he grabs me by the arm.

Up until this point in my life, he, nor any other man has ever grabbed me before. He's a very strong, and physically dominating person. The way he grabs me sends another powerful wave of fear down my body. He has pulled me so hard that it takes a little bit of my breath away. I'm pushing him away as hard as I can and telling him that he's hurting me, but I'm no match against him.

(I can sense that he's done this to women in the past, and he's letting me know that this is how he operates, especially when it comes to women.)

"What is wrong with you?" I keep asking him. "We are in front of the courthouse." I feel like I'm watching a scene play out between two strangers, like part of me left my body and is watching this drama as a third party. He shakes me then one last time really hard and lets me go. At this point I hate him, and I know that he's crazy. He's clearly telling me that no court order will stop him.

"I'm going to marry you," he's saying to me. "We're supposed to be together." He's saying all kinds of stuff like that.

"I don't want to be with you," I tell him. "We are over. You need to move on." He keeps talking for a few minutes, and I just keep saying I don't want to be with him. Eventually, he leaves me alone.

I'm in such shock that I just sit down on a bench in front of the courthouse and take some deep breaths as he walks away and heads toward the parking lot . When I'm breathing a little easier, I call my father, and I tell him everything that's happening. I'm so scared, shaken, and shocked by the experience that I can't even cry.

After about twenty minutes, I get off the phone with my dad, and I just sit on the bench in a daze. I look to my left, and I notice that a security guard has come out to see if things are okay. Apparently someone told him that two people were outside arguing. The security guard takes a quick glance around and goes back inside the building. I want to shout, "Somebody help me!" But I can't move. I can't talk. All I can do is sit in utter disbelief.

Almost like clockwork, as soon as the security guard goes back inside the building, I look to my right and see "monster" walking toward me. He's carrying two plastic bags in his hand. One's pink and the other's white. What the hell is he doing? I think to myself. I still can't move any part of my body—it's as if I'm completely frozen. What does he want now?

He comes over to me and says, "I got you something." Again, it's as if we're in this happy, healthy relationship, as if we weren't just in front of a judge for a restraining order, as if he hadn't just shaken me thirty minutes ago. He opens the pink plastic bag and says something like I got you a scarf and this and that, etc.

He's pulling out all of these little gifts, and I keep saying, "I don't want anything from you." He ignores what I say, though, and keeps calling me "baby." It's as if in his mind he doesn't realize that anything is wrong. I refuse to even touch anything, so he sits the pink bag on my lap. I take it off my lap and place it on the space next to me. I can tell he's start-ing to get annoyed.

"Why are you being so mean to me?" he asks.

Finally, I can move. I feel my feet kind of tingle again, let-ting me know that I'm ready to walk. In that second, I stand up and start walking toward the stairs to the parking garage. He runs in front of me. When I get to the second floor of the garage, he's already at my car, and he's placed the bag on my car. He's blocking the driver's door to my car, standing there, making me promise that I'll take his "gift."

I agreed in order to get him out of my way then I unlock my door and get into the car. Once I'm in the car, I throw the bag out and speed off. My father calls me and lets me know that the monster has called him three times, back to back too. That night, the phone calls intensify. It's as if the restraining order has fed his need to let me know that nothing is going to stop him.

October 2008

Today is October 3rd, and he's called me a record 35 times, going back and forth between my home phone to my cell phone. When I don't answer either one, he texts me. He calls me so much that I don't understand how he has time to do an-ything else. Each voicemail gets scarier and scarier. The an-ger in his voice—anger I've never heard from him before—is increasing. He's not cursing at me, but I can tell he wants to. His anger is very controlled—almost like he's about to snap.

I am inside my house, in my prayer room upstairs, shaking with fear. He's been stalking me for a while now, and I can feel his energy. It's very strong. It's violent. I don't know how else to explain it. It's as if he's become obsessed with me, and I can feel that obsession. I can feel his thoughts and frustration that I'm not giving in to him. He's angry that I won't take his calls. I can feel it, and I am terrified. My whole body shakes, and I have this nervous feeling in my stomach, like I'm going to throw up.

I sense that he's in my neighborhood even though when I look out the window, I don't see him anywhere. He's been calling me all day, saying something about his job. It's 3:15 p.m. and someone's knocking at my door. Oh my God, it's him. Fear rushes down my entire body again. The knocking turns to banging. This time when I look out the window from my upstairs room, I can see his car parked directly in front of my house. I walk to the bottom of the stairs, and I can hear him banging on the door, telling me he knows I'm in here. I sit at the bottom of the stairs and cry silently. I am so afraid, and I don't know what to do.

I call the police, and when they get to my house, he's gone. They can't find him anywhere in the neighborhood. I'm really feeling like the officers aren't taking the incident seriously. One of them tells me to go back to court and file a document stating that he has violated the restraining order. For the first time, I feel helpless.

I can't stay at my house tonight, so I decide to spend the night at a friend's house. I am so nervous and so shaken. I'm restless. I don't sleep anymore because I'm always afraid that something's going to happen. I don't know what it is yet, but the "It" is coming. I need to try and get some rest, so once I'm at Jennie's house, I turn off my phone. It feels so good to be away from my home. He's never met Jennie, and he has no idea where she lives, so I feel a little safe - at least for tonight.

I wake up at 6:30 a.m. I turn on my phone, and it's already ringing. When I look in the mirror, I see my eyes are blood-shot and puffy from all the crying and lack of sleep. My hair looks crazy. And there's fear in my eyes. I'm still shaking, but I know it's time to go home. Jennie tells me I can stay for as long as I need to, but I'm tired of running. I've stayed with different friends lately, and I'm just tired of it. I pray to God for protection and mercy, and Jennie drives me back to my house at about 7:15 a.m.

As soon as we pull into my development, I see him. He parked his car all the way down the street so that I couldn't possibly see him from my window. He's obviously just parked his car and is walking toward my house, looking very suspicious. Another chill goes down my body. I can't be-lieve he's doing this—he was just at my house less than twenty-four hours ago. I look at Jennie and her disbelief mir-rors my own. All I can think is that he must have some time off of work, and he's going to harass me all day long. I now see him as a monster, that thing under the bed when you're little. He represents something horrible, taunting, and so dis-ruptive to my life. I feel that I'm losing the sense of peace and tranquility that I have strived so hard to maintain in my work, home, and life in general.

I decide to tell Carlton, one of my neighbors, what's going on. That way he can also help me watch out for this guy.

I am so tired of running. My friends know this and give me all kinds of advice. Some tell me to move back to California or just move, period. But I don't want to move. I've just started my business, and I own my home. It's not that easy to just pick up and move. Plus, I know in my heart that he's so obsessed with me that somehow he will find me no matter where I go. In this day and age, anybody can find you. I've never been this stressed, scared, and confused in my entire life .

I know that he's found new ways to spy on me because every time I walk in the door, my home phone rings. It never fails—it's like clockwork. I changed the locks on my doors because he sent me a message claiming that he has a copy of my keys. I installed a new alarm system too. Despite all of this, I never feel safe—even when the police come by. He's smart enough to know how to disappear before they show up. He also likes to send me text messages telling me he saw some of the kids in my neighborhood doing something near my home. It's very passive-aggressive behavior, but he's letting me know that he's watching me.

The interesting thing is that he never really raises his voice on the messages. A lot of times he even starts off as if we're still in a relationship and he just wants to talk. Then he sounds irritated—but still calm—saying he just wants to hear my voice. Then he starts with the pleas:

"Just let me know if you're seeing someone else, and I'll stop calling you."

Then there are other messages that let me know he's watching me. That he's in control. That I can't run. That he'll win me back.

"Yeah, I'm thinking about moving to the Bay Area. I've already applied to some schools out there." He knows that's where my family is, that it's the most likely place I'd seek some refuge.

In October 2008 I am rarely at my own house. I stay with

friends for days at a time. I'm angry because I can't rest. I can't focus on my new business. I have no peace. All I have is fear and the knowledge deep inside me that something bad is about to happen and that no one will be able to stop it or protect me.

For now, I'm staying a half an hour away with Charisse, another one of my good friends. He doesn't know her or where she lives. Part of me feels guilty and a little ashamed to have to involve my friends in my personal drama, but I really don't know what else to do. I've already missed a couple of friends' birthday parties and celebrations because I was terrified to leave the house or because I felt sick.

I live with a nervous knot in my stomach—an unsettled feeling that I can't shake. I never sleep anymore, so I've trained my body to take thirty- or forty-minute naps throughout the day and night. I'm living a nightmare, and on top of everything, I swear I can feel all of his thoughts. I can sense now that he hates me even though he leaves me messages saying he doesn't hate me for filing the restraining order and that he loves me and wants to be with me. He says these things as if we have a normal relationship—as if everyone has this level of drama in their lives. No matter how strong I try to be, I am afraid.

While I am staying with my friend, he continues to call. Then he has one of his friends call me, and his friend offers to talk to me about monster's and my problems. I really can't believe this. I don't know what version of this experience monster has shared with his friend, but his attempt at an intervention is definitely annoying.

January, 14, 2009

Wednesday, January 14, 2009, is quiet and still and ... different. A lot of emotions are running around inside me. I'm restless, distracted, worried, anxious, sad, frustrated—and I'm scared.

I am extremely exhausted and have big bags under my eyes because I haven't been sleeping for the past five months. No longer comfortable in my own home, I sleep with a large knife under my pillow because I think that he's going to break in when I'm not here and hide in my closet or something. I filed the restraining order against him, and that didn't stop any of his activity. Actually it's gotten worse. After suffering for months like this, it's taken a toll on my health and energy. I'm not sleeping, and most days, I don't really have an appetite. He sees me as his prey—and that's how I feel.

I'm working on a big presentation that I have to deliver in two weeks, but I just can't concentrate. I've decided to let the weird mix of emotions come and go as they need to, supporting myself along the way with a heartfelt prayer or a quick meditation to center me. My spirit is very alive, and it guides me in what I need to do.

Nurture yourself, I think. So, I decide to cook one of my favorite meals: chicken tacos with Spanish rice, homemade guacamole, and refried beans. I sit at my kitchen table in complete silence, feeling more settled but still nervous and a bit anxious. I take a relaxing bubble bath and just soak in the water, connecting to God.

As I prepare to go to a class at church, I have the sense that I'm preparing for something—something more than church. At church, I catch up with friends, but I still don't feel like myself. I'm talkative, but at the same time, an uncomfortable uneasiness takes me over. I brush it off and focus instead on the class at church. My intuition is speaking to me loudly, I know that, but I'm not sure what I'm hearing. I've spent the past five months worrying and being afraid of something bad happening—a fear I've never had in my life. But this time, things feel really, really strange. I just can't put my finger on it.

The drive home from church is different too. The familiar, thirty-minute drive seems to go in slow motion. Why can't I just relax my mind? I think. Why have I been sad for no apparent reason lately and crying more than normal? It's a cold January evening, and I can't wait to get inside my warm home. As I exit the interstate and make the usual right turn at the light in front of my development, I hear a voice so clearly say, "He's here."

What? I think. I immediately dismiss the thought and, as I make the second right turn into my development, I say out loud to myself, "That can't be true." As I park in front of my home, I'm very uncomfortable. It's approximately 9:55 p.m., and I sit in the car for a few moments to collect myself. I'm nauseous, and I'm burning up on the inside despite the freezing cold January temperature. I need these precious few moments, even though at this moment, I don't know why. I get out of the car, take a deep breath, and lock the car door. As I walk toward the six steps leading to my front door, I hear a familiar voice.

"Soyini."

I know this voice—it's haunted me for months. A chill of absolute fear runs down my spine, and I begin to shake uncontrollably. My heart pounds so hard that I come to understand the phrase, "beating outside of my chest." My stomach spins and turns. I feel like I'm running on the inside. This is it, I think. My worst nightmare is about to come true.

I stand there on the sidewalk in total shock. I can't believe he's here in front of me; it's been months since I've seen him. I'm absolutely terrified. I look down at my right hand. I'm holding the materials from church, and my hand is shaking uncontrollably. Oh God, I can't believe this.

"What are you doing here? You're not supposed to be here," I say to him. I'm so scared.

"We need to talk," he says and very forcefully grabs and jerks my left arm.

At this point, I'm beyond terrified. My fear is absolute, and I'm afraid for my life. I can't believe this is happening. My feet are cemented to the ground. I am so terrified that I literally can't move my feet. I want to turn around and run as fast as I can, but I'm paralyzed by my fear.

"I'm scared!" I blurt out. I can no longer control my inner dialogue because of the fear living inside of me. I sense that he likes the fact that I'm afraid—it gives him a sense of control, and he likes that.

His massive, six-foot five-inch frame towers over me. I'm beyond intimidated. He is physically the same person, but there is something about his spirit that tells me that I need to be afraid for my life. As he pushes and shoves me up the six stairs to my door, his voice is hurried, and he gets more impatient by the second, insisting we talk. It's as if he has a task to carry out and I'm delaying his progress.

His eyes are dark, empty and hollow. As if all of life has been sucked out of his soul and left only two eyeballs with no contact to God or spirit. He wears a black New York Yankees baseball hat and jacket, over-sized grey sweat pants, and white sneakers. He smells of alcohol and something else I can't identify. Drugs? I have never smelled a smell like that. It smells like death. His eyes are dark, empty, and hollow, as if all of the life has been sucked out of his soul, leaving him with no contact to God and no spirit at all. Although he is familiar, there is an energy about him I don't recognize. Who is this stranger in front of me? All I know is that I'm looking at pure evil.

Because he's rushed me up to my door with my keys in my right hand, I automatically put the key into the door, preparing to turn the bottom lock. He is standing on my left and grabs my left arm, pushing me to get into the house. Everything is happening so fast, but instinctively I know it's a bad idea to let him into my home. He's really angry and he's taking control—rushing me and making sure I can't think straight. He knows I live alone, and if anything happens to me, it might be days before anyone notices that I've disappeared.

Nervously I ask, "Have you been drinking?" My house key is in the lock and my hand is on the key, preparing to unlock the door.

"No, no. Come on, let's go inside and talk," he says, yanking my left arm and trying to push me through my closed door.

Without turning the key in the lock, I look down and notice a huge bulge in his jacket pocket. I know he owns a gun— it's always made me uncomfortable. I remember he spent several years in the military and knows how to use any type of firearm.

My intuition speaks to me: He has a gun. He's here to kill me.

I look up at him and ask, "What's in your pocket?"

"It's just keys. Don't worry about it. Let's go in," he says casually as if it's normal for him to be at my house. As if all of this is normal.

At this point, God begins speaking to me rapidly. Some people might refer to this voice as Jesus, Allah, Buddha, Spirit, intuition, or simply my survival instinct. For me, it's the voice of God, and it's here to protect me. Thoughts and guidance come to me rapidly. It all happens so quickly that I don't even have time to pray. For months, I've known this man was up to something, but in my wildest dreams, I never thought that it would end like this.

I quickly take the key out of the door. As I remove the key from the door, fear begins to leave my spirit and courage steps in. (Looking back, I think this is the one decision that definitely saved my life. I lived alone. There's no telling what would have happened if he'd gotten me into the house. I could have lain dead in my house for days before anyone discovered me. I get chills every time I think about it.)

Someone's going to die tonight—either me or this mother&%@&%$—and it ain't gonna be me, I think to myself. I know in my heart that we both aren't leaving here alive. All of these months of fear and terror have come down to this one moment, late at night, on Wednesday, January 14, 2009. This is surreal.

As I have that thought, it's as if a light switch inside of me flips on. I've been the victim for several months now, and I'm damn tired of it. I immediately pull the key out of the lock and turn and look him in the eyes.

"Whatever you have to say to me, you need to say it right here."

With the key out of the door, I am no longer afraid. I am so bold now. I can tell my change in spirit has shocked and surprised him. My sudden strength catches him off guard. He's losing control, and he knows it.

At that point I look up and notice my neighbor directly across the street staring at us, trying to figure out the commotion. I'm certain she doesn't know what's going on. I want to shout and tell her my life's in danger, but I'm careful with every move that I make. I don't want to alarm this man.

I begin walking back down the stairs, and he follows me. I'm no longer afraid. I'm ready to confront this, and I'm surprised at myself. My voice goes from shaky and weak, to bold and powerful. I am tired of running. This has to stop.

"You're ruining my life," he says. "We need to talk."

I say nothing.

"You know I just lost my job," he continues. "If we go back to court, my life's going to be over. I just want to talk to you. Why are you acting like this?"

"I don't want to be in a relationship with you anymore," I say. "You need to move on. You're scaring me. Why can't you just leave me alone? I just want this relationship to be over." I reach the bottom of the stairs and turn right to go to my next-door neighbor's house for help.

I don't know it at the time, but his last words to me are, "I can't go to court—you know I have a son."

"Well, act like it."

My back is turned to him, and as I turn around to look at him, I see him quickly and angrily pull out a shiny, silver gun. I'm so shocked I'm not even sure whether or not I scream.

The first bullet hits me in the face and it stings, like when you get your ear pierced, but a thousand times more painful than that. As I fall to the ground, I realize I've been shot twice. The second bullet burns like fire as it passes through me. I can't believe any of this.

Somewhere in this moment, as I'm falling face forward toward the cement, I catch one last glimpse of him. I see him holding the gun and shooting it. I see a look of shock pass over his face as he realizes he's shot me. It's as if he was crazy and the sound of the gunshot snapped him back to reality. He looks scared, and then he turns and runs away to his truck. As I hit the cold cement, all I can think is God, this can't be the way I'm going to leave here.

I hear God's response so clearly, I can't mistake it. His answer, "It's not your time," comes thru my spirit, and I know that, no matter what happens next, I'm going to be here. I'm not ready to go, and most importantly, God isn't ready for me to go either.

I've fallen forward from the two gunshot wounds to my face, and I lie paralyzed on the cold January cement bleeding from my head. I feel an electric shock run throughout my body, and it seems like I'm bleeding everywhere. I'm scared that he shot me in the back, too, because I can't move.

My neighbors are screaming and crying.

"Oh my God!"

"Oh my God, Soyini!"

I hear lots of screaming and people praying over me. I hear people rushing to call the ambulance and police, but I can't see anything—I'm covered with blood.

I feel myself going into shock, and I sense my neighbors'

terror and disbelief. Then something magical happens.

I feel a presence under and around me. It isn't people. It feels like Angels. I can't see anything, but the energy—the feeling around me—is very powerful. It's as if Angels are lying under me, attempting to push me up and lift me off the cement. When I feel this presence, I begin pushing myself up too. My neighbor Carlton tells me to relax and not to move. I wonder why Carlton doesn't see the Angels lifting me up. I feel them so strongly, I'm sure someone else can see them too.

At the same time I'm angry. If I can get off the ground, I'm going to kick his a$$! I can't believe someone would do this to me. How did this happen to me—a woman who has always remained great friends with her ex-boyfriends? A woman who just wanted out of a relationship that no longer worked. Why wasn't it all over when it was over? Why did I become his obsession? Why did he accuse me of ruining his life when he was trying to ruin mine? None of this makes sense.

The human mind is interesting. I know that I've been shot, but my mind brings me back to the moment when I was going to enter my home. In my mind right now, I'm in my PJs, lying in my bed as if it's a normal Wednesday night. Part of me wonders how I got here in my bed. The other, more traumatized part of me knows I've just been shot and left for dead.

Oh my God, where did he go? He's going to realize he didn't finish the job, I think, and fear paralyzes me. I focus on moving my body, but I can't. Why can't I move? Why can't I open my eyes? For the next few seconds I focus on trying to regain control of my body. I'm frustrated because no matter how hard I try to move, I can't, and I can't see anything. I'm so scared. Then I feel a presence next to me, and I hear an unfamiliar female voice.

"Oh my God, honey, are you okay?" She sounds worried and very concerned, like a caring mother. I can tell that she's frantic, but she's trying to sound a little composed so as to not startle me too much.

I can't speak, but for some reason I can now nod my head yes. I wonder who this woman is and how she got into my house. I hear her talking to some other people, but I can't make out what she's saying, and I can't see anything. I am terrified, and I feel so alone.

Then I think to myself, Oh God! He's probably standing right next to her waiting to finish the job. In my mind, I can just imagine him standing there silently, focusing on me, waiting for the perfect time to complete his attack. Then I hear the woman's voice again.

"Oh my God, honey, are you in any pain?" I'm afraid, and I nod my head to signal, Yes, I'm in pain. I don't want my attacker to think that I'm not in pain for fear he might want to cause me even more harm than he already has.

Surprisingly though, I'm not in any physical pain at all. As unbelievable as it may sound, I felt the actual bullets pierce my face, but I'm in more emotional pain than anything else right now.

I hear this woman praying over me, but I really can't make out what she's saying. I sense a lot of panic, chaos, and confusion around me. At this point, my concern is that these voices I hear around me might be his friends—maybe they're here to trick me. I don't know what to do. I can still hear the woman and a few other unfamiliar voices, but I don't understand what's happening around me. Why are all of these people in my house?

All of the sudden, someone is tugging at my pant legs, as if they're trying to pull my jeans down. I'm terrified! I can't see who's doing any of this. I can't speak, I can't move, I can't see. I can't do anything but lie there in complete terror; wondering what's going to happen next. Oh my God, he's going to rape me! I want to scream for help! I want to cry! But I can't do anything. I know he's going to rape me before he kills me, and it's all just too painful for me. At this point, I just want to escape. I don't want to feel anything else.

This is where the sequence of events gets confusing because now I hear an unfamiliar male voice. I can tell that I'm not in my bed anymore. I know that I've been shot, but I don't think I've been raped. At this point, I begin to mentally detach from the experience—I stop thinking about it—to protect my own soul.

I focus on what's going on around me, and I can tell that I'm sitting up in some kind of chair or something. Then a man begins asking me a series of questions. I can't see him, but I sense that he's a police officer. Actually, I think he told me that, but I was so overwhelmed I didn't know what was going on.

"Ma'am, can you please give me your name?"

"Soyini Taylor."

"Do you know who did this to you?"

"Yes. His name is—" and I provide my attacker's phone number, address, and vehicle/license plate number. I also tell the officer about the restraining order and that I just got home from church. I explain everything that happened.

"Okay, Ms. Taylor, can you give me your relatives' phone number?"

I provide my mother's cell, work, and home number, and

the questions go on and on, and I talk for as long as I can. I'm so overwhelmed, confused, frustrated, and afraid, but my innermost thought and prayer is that if I die, I want my parents and everyone else to know exactly what happened to me.

It is not until much later that I realize that the lady around me was one of the paramedics on site.

January 15, 2009

I wake up and I'm in a hospital room with tubes coming out of me from everywhere. I've never been in the hospital in my whole life. Thank God—it's not like I've seen on TV. I'm in a small hospital room by myself, but I'm aware that there are other people around me. My bed is small; if I was a few inches taller, my feet would be hanging off the end of the bed. Oddly enough, I feel no pain.

I'm wearing a hospital gown. As I look around, I see there is no mirror in the room—only supplies for the doctor. I have a tube in my mouth that feels like it's connected to my head, and a bandage is wrapped around my head. My right eye is patched up, but I can see out of my left eye, so I look down at my hands and see they are extremely swollen. My nails have dried blood underneath them. My head itches, so I scratch it and notice that this is the reason for the dried blood under my nails. I continue my inventory of my body, scrolling down the length of it with my left eye to discover that I have some kind of grey legging things on my legs. My feet look the same, with the fresh pedicure I gave myself two nights ago. Was that really only two nights ago?

I have been through a lot in the last twenty-four hours, and my body feels the stress of it, yet there isn't the level of physical pain that I would expect. As I lay in the bed putting together the puzzle pieces of this nightmare, I realize that my nurse, Tasha, has come in to check on me. She has the sweetest voice—it's angelic, and I immediately feel more relaxed in her presence.

"Are you in any pain?" she asks. I open my mouth to tell her "No," but I quickly realize that the tube in my mouth prevents me from speaking, so I shake my head no instead. I fight the urge to gag from the pain and the discomfort of the tube in my throat, but I feel like I'm going to throw up. Tasha helps me calm down by giving me the best news of the day—my parents have been contacted and they will be here later on this evening. They are flying in from the West Coast. I'm so excited, but all I can do is smile. She tells me that I have lots of friends outside waiting for me, but before I can learn who is here, I fall into a deep sleep.

Next thing I know, I awaken to my mother's and father's voices. I'm so happy they're here. I can't really see them, and I can't talk because of the ridiculously long tube down my throat, so I decide to communicate with my hands and my head. Using my sense of sound I determine how close my mother is to me, and I grab her hand in a way that says, "Mommy, I'm scared and I am so glad you're here." She talks to me and tells me my oldest brother, Dwayne will be flying in tonight from Montreal, Canada. Yes, my family is scattered all around the world, but we are exceptionally close. My father sits next to my mother, and I can feel how glad he is that I'm alive. I feel very safe. I sense my parents' relief that my condition isn't as bad as they'd feared.

My other close friends are also here. They picked my parents up from the airport and drove them to the hospital to be with me. I am engulfed by love. I feel the prayers of many people surrounding me. I can't really see, but I can sense all of their positive energy.

My nurse lets me know that the visiting room is also full of guests for me. My aunt Bonnie and my cousin have come up from Virginia, and they brought food for everyone and a Bible for me. Now I can hear all the voices in the visiting room, and I want to be out there in the "party." Guests keep coming into my room. My nurse tells me that I must be very popular because she has never seen anyone with so many visitors. When I'm awake, I have very little time alone. Someone is always in the room with me, keeping me company. I feel a little bad saying it, but I'm tired of guests. I appreciate the love, but it still hurts to attempt to talk, and my energy feels drained.

Then my brother arrives! I'm so happy to see him. He and my mother read me stories from the Bible, and they read me some of Aesop's fables. At this point, I'm not even listening to their words—I'm just happy to hear their voices.

It seems as though doctors are in and out of the room checking on me every hour. They check my vitals and my eyes. They ask about my pain level. After they leave, I go back into a deep, uninterrupted sleep. I keep thinking, How many doctors are involved here? I've never seen this many doctors and specialists in my entire life.

Through all of this, I feel exceptionally connected with God. Even though I'm extremely exhausted, my connection to God is stronger than it's ever been before. I've always had a strong connection to God, but now I feel like we have a "Relationship." In all of the chaos, there is a stillness inside me that I've never felt in my life. I literally feel God's hand on me. It's an experience I'll never be able to put into words—there aren't words to describe it. I hear God telling me to relax and remain calm, that everything is going to be okay. I feel so loved! There aren't many people who can say that they feel God that intimately.

I'm not sure what day it is, but I wake up thinking, I wonder what happened to the psycho that did this to me? When I have the thought, one of my closest friends is in the room. I had dreamt that I wrote him a letter telling him I forgive him for what he did to me. I know that thought had to come from God because I'm not sure I'd be capable of coming to that understanding so quickly on my own. I try to ask my friend Tonia, "How can I ever forgive him for doing this to me?" but my voice is very weak at this point. All of the surgeries I've had over the past few days, the massive blood loss, and no food or drink in days have left me physically exhausted.

She thinks I'm asking for water. I shake my head no, a little frustrated, so she hands me a note pad and pencil and asks me to write down my question. I grab the pencil, but my swollen hands and fingers prevent me from writing anything short of chicken scratches. Oh well, visiting hours are over, and it's time for me to get some rest. The question of forgiveness can wait.

I wake up again with no idea what day it is. Doctors always ask me if I know where I am. "University of Maryland Medical Center," I answer in the strongest voice possible.

"Are you in any pain?"

"No." I'm still amazed at what God can do.

"Do you know what day it is?" I reach back into my mental Rolodex and tell them that it's probably January 16th or something. I tell them I've lost track of the days, but I guess my answers are good enough.

The doctors explain that my right eye needs to be removed. They explain in detail what might happen to my good eye if I leave the damaged eye in. For me, the choice is very simple—I have no intention of being blind. Thank God, I've always had great eyesight, and I have two eyes. It was an easy choice. I wish I didn't have to lose anything, but all I can think is that I'm just happy to be alive.

More visitors come and I get more rest. The prayers are coming in so strong. I feel like the entire world is praying for me. Prayer really works, I think to myself.

Unfortunately, the prayers don't help my comfort or my hunger. The hospital bed isn't soft and cushy like my bed at home. I adjust myself in the bed, squirming around to try to find the best, most comfortable position. Unable to find one and feeling tired, I stop and settle exactly where I am. I naively ask my nurse for something to eat, but she lovingly informs me that I have surgery in a few days and my stomach needs to be empty. I want to cry. The whole time I've been here, I've had nothing to eat. Oh well, life goes on.

Wow, today is inauguration day! Go Obama. I was scheduled to be a volunteer on the National Mall for this historic event, but I can't go because I'm going into surgery. It's funny, there is an old saying that says something to the effect of We plan and God laughs. So true. I had the whole year planned out—this was my year for Change!

This change isn't quite what I expected.

Today's surgery is different because I have absolutely no memory of the other surgeries that I've undergone, but for this one I am aware. My nurse preps me for surgery, and then we head out of my room. While we're on the elevator, I think, "Wow, I can't believe I'm getting my eye removed." Actually the medical term is enucleated.

As I arrive in the operating room, I have lots of nurses and doctors asking me if I have any questions, but I don't, and besides, I can't talk easily. Even though the tube has been removed, when I try to talk, I choke and gag. It feels like I'm going to cough up my insides.

Next, they roll me into the actual operating room. For a few minutes I'm in front of a stainless steel paper towel dispenser, which has a mirror-like surface. For the first time in almost a week since everything happened, I catch a glimpse of myself. My face is really swollen, and my head is shaved in the front around my hairline. Wow, I think, if that's what I look like, thank God they don't have mirrors in the hospital room. Then the anesthesiologist comes in and it's lights out for me.

As I come to, I'm asked the familiar questions again: "Are you in any pain? Do you know what today is?" I feel simply like I took a long sleep. They push me to my new room. I won't see my old nurse again, but my new nurse is also attentive, and I go back to sleep.

My parents and brother are in the room the next time I wake. I feel a little more energetic. My voice is still very weak, but now I'm able to speak a few words without coughing and gagging so much. I should be out of the hospital in a couple of days, and I can't wait. I'm hungry and I miss my bed. I just want to go home.

Lots more of my friends come to visit, and I now have a TV in my room. I know a TV seems like a small thing, but any semblance of normal life becomes increasingly important. My friend Donna and her husband Pete have driven down from Pennsylvania to Baltimore, and brought me a Washington Post newspaper featuring the Inauguration coverage of our newly elected president. More flowers, teddy bears, and cards are sent to my room, and I'm very appreciative of the love shown by family, friends, and even people who have just heard about my situation.

Before they release me from the hospital, I have to do physical therapy. I've been bedridden for days, and my balance is off because of my enucleated eye, so I have to learn to walk again. There are only a few hundred feet between my hospital room and the end of the hall, but I'm so exhausted that I can barely make the walk without stopping every few steps to get some more strength. Because I don't do well on this first walking test, I have to repeat it in a few days. I also have to see a specialist about my ability to swallow food. My jaw is fractured, so the doctors want to make sure that I'll be okay. It's such a relief to be able to eat and drink again. I don't think I've ever been so happy to have a few graham crackers and apple juice in my life.

I'm resting in my hospital room, while my dad and my brother are in the room with me, and my mother is taking a nap in the visitors' room. It feels so good when I wake up and see my family or friends standing by my bedside. I've been having nightmares, so I ask my dad and my brother to sleep in the room with me. Their presence makes me feel safe, and I sleep better.

In the moments that I have alone with my dad and my brother, I have the chance to ask what happened to "him."

"Are you sure you want to know?," my dad is saying in a concerned tone.

"Yeah"

It was then that I found out that shortly after shooting me, he had driven a few miles away and ended his own life. I felt some relief, and was able to sleep a little easier. I still had nightmares, but not as many as before.

I continue to feel the prayers from family, friends, and my church family. I've always known that I was a social person, but up until now I never realized how many strong connections I've made with people. I have always believed that it's very important to invest in your friendships with people and to touch lives. It's amazing how tragedy brings folks closer, and people begin to share feelings about you that they don't normally speak.

Today it's time to check out of the hospital, and I'm starving. I guess that's a good sign that I'm getting my strength back. I don't eat beef, but right now I feel like eating a huge, juicy steak and a buttery baked potato.

I sign my discharge papers and thank the nurses. My voice is coming back a little more. Each day I feel just a small bit of strength returning. For the first time in my life, I sit in a wheelchair, and I'm rolled out of the hospital room downstairs to the car. I've had some excellent medical attention, but I'm ready to be in my "own" bed and eat real food.

My family takes me to a hotel because I'm too afraid to go to my house. It's an official crime scene and a chilling reminder of the events that occurred last week. When we arrive at the hotel, my two brothers (Dwayne and Eric), my dad, and my mom help me out of the car because I'm so weak and drowsy from all the medications at the hospital. Our room is only on the second floor, but it felt like I had to walk up a flight of 100 stairs to get there. I kept saying God, please let me get to the top of the stairs without falling. I was exhausted. Although I'm a young, athletic woman who has run two half-marathons—not tooting my own horn, but trying to make a point—I currently have the strength of an 80-year-old woman.

When I make it into the hotel room, my mom tells me, "Sit down and rest, sweetheart." She can clearly see the extent of the physical challenge I've just experienced.

When I look at my family, I see a weird mix of emotions.

My mother's strength and love are apparent, but I also see a lot of fear and disbelief in her. My father looks tired, but his love is also clear. He looks relieved that he still has me here—he knew every single detail that happened over the past four months before this tragedy. My brothers are also shaken—they can't believe their big sister has endured so much.

At this point, I decide it's time to take a bath. It's been about a week, and those hospital sponge baths just didn't do it for me. My mother runs my bath water and helps me get into the bath tub, and I flashback to being a toddler and having Mom bathe me. Who would have ever thought that when I was 34 years old, Mom would be doing it again?

After the bath, I get out and decide that I want to see what I look like. Since everything happened, I've only had one quick glimpse of myself in the reflection of the paper towel dispenser in the operating room. Now, I figure it's time for my close-up. In the hospital, I heard family and friends say, "Oh my God, she looks like herself," or "Thank God, she still has her beauty," and my girlfriends saying, "Oh, she just had a pedicure! Look at our girl!" And we all laughed. Looking back, I appreciated comments that made me laugh and lightened the mood for all of us, like when all of the nurses would tell me how great I looked even though it was obvious that something was different. Well, I need to see for myself.

So, with my PJs on and very little energy, I stand in front of the mirror for the first time. The first thing I notice is how thin I've gotten. I've always been a curvy girl—I exercised regularly and ate a good diet. I took care of myself. I looked "healthy." Now, I'm a lot thinner, maybe ten to fifteen pounds lighter, it's hard to say.

I see little prick marks on my stomach from all of the shots

I had there. It seems like every day, nurses would say, "Okay, honey, we have to give you a shot in your stomach. Is that okay?" Of course I couldn't say no. I was proud of being such a good patient, always cooperating because I wanted everything to work out. Before this experience, I hated getting shots. The thought of needles sent me into a state of panic. But fortunately or unfortunately, I'm no longer afraid of needles.

Next, I look down at my left arm where the IV fed me. My arm is full of little prick marks, and it's a little black and blue from all the shots and the blood that the nurses drew over the past week. I scroll down to my hand, and there are tiny prick marks there, too. My fingernails are clean, and there is no more dried blood underneath them. I direct my eyes up without looking too much at my face. I see the area right below my left collar bone—all these little prick marks. Now, after taking myself in bit by bit, I'm ready for the real image.

I purposely look directly in the mirror at my face. The first thing that stands out is my right eye. There is a huge white patch of gauze taped on it from the surgery I had a few days ago. Then I see my head and where my hairline was completely shaved from ear to ear. There is a two-inch strip that begins at my hairline where I'm completely bald, although the rest of my hair is there—and it's very curly because it had been drenched in blood a week ago. I also see a tiny, meticulous line of stitches across my head from ear to ear, but you know what? I look like me.

My face is puffy, and my cheeks are sticking out. This helps explain why I had such a hard time speaking. Other than this, my face looks the same—same nose, chin, everything. Underneath my chin is a gauze bandage covering up a hematoma. I had never heard of a hematoma before, but I learned that it's basically a blood clot and it will drain. I notice my complexion is very pale, which I would later find out is because I lost such a massive amount of blood.

My reflection in the mirror shows me a woman who will never be the same again, even though I basically still look like the old me. The whole experience has been surreal. Exhausted, I decide it's time for me to go to bed.

Over the next few days I wake up from my naps and pinch myself to see if I'm really still here. I can't believe that I'm up moving around days after such a great tragedy. My outlook on life is shifting. I used to worry about and fear so many things in life. Now I understand what a waste of time that is.

My look changes every day. Today I'm still very frail and pale. My energy isn't where it used to be, but I can walk a few more steps longer before I have to sit down and take a breath. There really isn't any physical pain, and the idea that I feel relatively the same astonishes me and my family and friends.

My phone and my parents' phone ring off the hook as people call in their prayers and condolences. I can't tell you how many times I've heard variations of the phrase, "If there's anything I can do, please let me know."

I contact the local police department to arrange to pick up my personal items they kept after the shooting . When I contact the detective, his disbelief is apparent. He keeps asking me, "Who is this again?" as if he can't believe that we're talking two weeks after the shooting.

I've never been to a police station in my life, so my brother Dwayne takes me there. It's a cold January afternoon and there's still snow on the ground. We park the car and my brother grabs my arm to support me. At times, my balance is off, so he wants to make sure that I don't slip and fall on the ice. (I often think that it would be ironic if I survived what would be anyone's worst nightmare and not feel any pain, but slip and fall and be bound to a wheelchair.)

We walk into my small-town police station that's only miles away from my home, and it's very quiet—nothing like the police departments I see on TV in New York City. I notice a receptionist's office to the rear of the building, so I walk over to her and tell her who I am and that I'm here to see Detective Hansen. While she contacts him, Dwayne and I wait on a small bench in the lobby.

When the detective walks out, he looks at me like he's seen a ghost. The last time he saw me, I was lying unconscious on the small hospital bed, fighting for my life. Now I'm standing in front of him in my favorite jeans, a hooded green sweater, and boots. My hair is still kind of all over the place because I didn't want to mess with the stitches, and my eye is still covered with an eye patch as it's still healing. I can see the genuine care and concern in the detective's eyes, and I can hear it in his voice. As I talk to Detective Hansen, I know that he's someone I will never forget.

He tells me that I'm such a fighter, that I have such a strong will to live. He tells me that I did everything that I could that night to stay alive. And he tells me that he's seen lots of cases similar to mine, and that often, in times of enormous tragedy and trauma, people simply lose the will to live. They stop fighting for their lives. But with me, he says I have a strong will to live.

"It's clear that you wanted to be here," he says to me. "That you wanted to be alive." He says he's just relieved that I'm standing in front of him, and I thank him for everything.

When Detective Hansen goes to retrieve my things, another

officer walks into the room. It's Officer Spencer, who was one of the first officers on the scene. He's the officer who was in the ambulance with me and kept me talking. He took all of my vital information and got my parents' info as well. I talked to him in the ambulance until I passed out, so I thank him too.

A third officer is also there, Officer Johnson, a very tall, athletic man with a quiet, observant disposition. He had been at the scene too. As I gather my purse, wallet, and personal items, I continue to thank all of them because each one of them helped me stay alive. As I leave the police station, I feel a sense of relief.

At this point, Dwayne says that we need to go do something fun, so we decide to go catch a movie and grab something to eat. I still don't have an appetite and my jaw is still giving me problems, so eating is the last thing on my mind. I watch my brother enjoy a hamburger, fries, and a milkshake, and I order a small bowl of soup and slowly sip on the broth.

Every time I'm out, I notice people looking at the patch on my right eye, my swollen face, the stitches around my hair line, and the gauze under my chin that is collecting the blood from the hematoma. I see the questions on their faces: "I wonder what happened to her?" Some people look at me with pity. As they notice me notice them, they smile and look away. I ignore the stares as much as possible.

As my brother and I walk into the movie theater, he says, as if he can read my mind , "Don't worry about them, Sis." So for the next two hours, while the movie plays, I just forget about everything that happened to me and I enjoy the time that I have with my brother.

As time goes by, I continue to adjust to things. My parents are with me, and I'm still uncomfortable being by myself—

not because I'm afraid, but because I need their care. I can no longer take care of myself. My parents have to drive me everywhere. They encourage me when I feel down. They get me food. I really need their love and support.

My friends are so important now too because they help me feel normal again. We reminisce about old times. We laugh and giggle, act silly, and gossip. My life just feels normal again when I have my friends with me. My friend Tonia always brings me the best homemade cupcakes. Andrea just makes me laugh. Yvonne is my spiritual sister. I can call any of my friends whenever I need to cry or talk, and they are always there, but Yvonne is the one I talk to regularly.

February 2009

Finally , I reach the point where the whole thing begins to sink in. A month after the shooting, I still don't have an appetite, but I drink a few protein shakes each day to restore nourishment to my body. As I lie in my bed, I smell dinner cooking downstairs. My parents are in the kitchen preparing something for me to eat. It smells yummy. It's as if my parents sent the aroma upstairs into my bedroom to lie right under my nose in hopes of bringing back my appetite.

I've received so many gifts and cards since I got out of the hospital, and one of my favorite gifts is a journal from my friend Tonia. It's beautiful; it's small with a Moroccan-looking print on the cover. Because she is one of my closest friends, Tonia knows how much I like to write. With my balance and sense of equilibrium slowly returning, I can finally hold a pen and write the way that I used to.

The first month out of the hospital has been hard—so many emotions to process. I still wake up every day and pinch myself to see if it was all a dream. Did I really get shot twice in the head face area and survive? My family and friends tell me how strong, powerful, and courageous I am which strikes me funny because I've never really seen myself that way.

I don't understand God anymore. It's as if everything that I thought about life and God changed in a matter of seconds. I pick up my pen, and all I can write are two words: "God. WHY?" I feel like the universe has played a bad joke on me. Why did something so tragic happen to me? I've never hurt anyone, and I've always felt that I've lived a good life. I was good to people.

My journal entry turns into a series of questions:

Why me?

What did I do wrong?

Where will I live?

What about my income?

Will I ever have sight in my right eye again?

Countless questions come to me, and I write as fast as I can, hoping that God will step in and write the answers. As the questions come, tears pour down my cheeks, and I realize that I'm grieving for the life I no longer have. My pain is deep.

"WHY GOD? WHY ME? WHAT DID I DO TO DE-SERVE THIS?" I'm giving voice to my pain, and I can hear it as I sob. I cry harder for myself and all that I've been through. I go through a whole box of tissues this evening, and I keep thinking, I don't know if I can do this. Can I go on? I'm not that strong.

When I look up, my parents are standing at my bedroom door, and I can see the pain in their eyes, too. It's torn them apart to see me go through this. They walk to my bed and sit next to me—my dad on the right of me and my mom on the left. They both hold me and hug me and kiss me as if I'm a little baby. Neither of them say anything; they just let me get my last few tears out.

Finally my father says, "It's going to get better, sweetheart."

"We are with you," Mom adds, and I feel safer than I've ever felt before. I feel like my parents have also been my angels.

The three of us get up and walk downstairs to the kitchen. I feel lighter after my good cry, but I still don't have much of an appetite. My jaw is still sore, so it's very difficult to open it up even to eat a small bite of anything. My mother brings me a plate with a small portion of things that I can eat—a small helping of mashed potatoes and a few vegetables that she's mashed up for me. Yes, I definitely feel like their little baby again—literally. I'm eating food all mashed up like a baby.

I'm at the pharmacy, picking up some ointment for my eye, and all I can think is, I hate him. I just hate him. As CJ, the pharmacist, rings me up, that thought circles through my brain. CJ is friendly and young—he looks like he's in his late 20s, possibly 27 or 28. He makes small talk with me as he rings me up, and I know that he senses I'm having a bad day. I swear, I didn't realize someone could really talk and maintain a smile the whole time.

I still have to wear this thing that I refer to as head gear, but the doctors call it a head dressing. I still have the blood clot in my jaw that needs to be bandaged to keep pressure on it, so the doctors placed a bandage literally around my entire head. In addition to that, I'm still wearing an eye patch over my eye, waiting for it to heal. So CJ must feel it's his duty to be pleasant no matter what.

"Okay, Miss Taylor, that will be $121.75," CJ says.

"What?" I ask. I have him repeat the total a few times to make sure that my ears are working properly—unfortunately, they are. Without insurance for the first time in my life, I realize how much I miss it. I'm living on savings, and I certainly don't have the money to dole out for this tiny tube of ointment. I quickly purchase the ointment and turn around and storm out of the pharmacy .

As I walk out, tears stream down my face. I hate crying in public, but I can't control these tears—they've been coming for a while. Although it's freezing outside, I'm burning up on the inside with so much anger at HIM. Why did he do this to me? He's still trying to ruin my life, I think to myself. I'm so angry. As I get into the car, I call my brother, but I wonder if I'm even going to be able to get the words out with the anger in the way.

I'm hyper-ventilating and praying that Dwayne will answer the phone because I really need to say those words out loud. On the second ring, my brother picks up and all I can blurt out is, "I Hate Him! I Hate Him so much!" And then come all of the tears and the sobbing, the familiar hurt and grief springing out of my deep sadness.

I tell my brother how upset I am and how much I hate that this happened, and I feel the heat in my body and the heaviness in my heart when I say the words I HATE HIM. My brother listens patiently and encourages me as I vent for about 15 minutes.

When we get off the phone, I feel lighter, and something (God) says to me: "Let it go." I realize, when I hear these words, that I need to forgive this man. I am physically and emotionally tired of the heaviness in my heart, so I decide to begin the process of forgiveness.

I'm definitely not saying that I'm some saint, and I'm not expecting this process of forgiveness to be easy. But I'm choosing to do something different. (I refer to this a *process* of forgiveness because you will see that I have had to do this numerous times.) Each time I forgive him, more of me opens up, as if I'm creating more space in my heart.

April 2009

It's April and I've gone back to the West Coast to stay with my parents. I still have days when I'm in a fog. I feel like I've lost complete control in my life. People keep asking me about my plans for the future, but I have absolutely no idea how to answer them. My life has been turned upside down. Every day I'm thankful to God for keeping me here—I understand that it's nothing short of a miracle. But for the first time in my adult life, I really have no idea what I'm going to do day to day. My mother gives me the best, most logical, simple advice: "Don't try to figure out life right now. Just take it one day at a time." And that's what I have to do; otherwise, I'm so overwhelmed that I probably wouldn't be able to get out of bed.

I write down a list of all the questions that I have for God, and I write them as if I have a meeting coming up with God where He will sit across from me and give me the answers, one by one. As I write, I trust that one day they will all be answered. I come up with a list of 30 good ones and transfer them into my journal, making sure that I leave enough space for God to answer. After I write them down, I realize there are about six or seven categories of questions that I've asked in different ways. Somehow, this makes me feel better. It's something about ideas and thoughts just floating loosely around in my head that I don't like. That confusion goes away when I sit down and write things out on paper.

Prior to the shooting, my whole life seemed to revolve around two key themes: finding and living my Purpose and finding Love. I never realized how much energy I put into those two areas of my life. The near loss of my life has refocused me in a powerful way .

One night, I feel this tremendous amount of Joy—Joy that I haven't felt in a long time. Something in my spirit feels very alive and free, and I have this total and complete feeling of self-love and acceptance that I've never felt before. Then a thought comes to me: Just to be alive is enough. So simple, yet so profound. I whip out my lifeline (my journal) and write it down in capital letters: JUST TO BE ALIVE IS ENOUGH. In a flash, I see how my whole self-worth has been tied up in those two areas of my life: Purpose and Love.

My mind quickly scans all of the good and not-so-good relationships that I've had over the years. Before the shooting, I felt so complete if I was in a relationship or about to enter into a relationship. I was always trying to find the perfect guy and the perfect relationship, or I was on the unrealized quest for my life's purpose. I had heard so many people over the years talk about their Purpose and how "you've gotta live your purpose."

Now, in my early 30s, as I lie in bed in my parents' home in my pink pajamas, sipping on green tea, I realize that I don't have either one of those "dreams" realized. But—and this is a big "but"—I totally love and accept myself. I've dropped the conditions that I had on my self-worth, and now I realize that Just to be alive is enough. I don't have to do or prove all of these things to God, myself, my family, my friends, or anyone else to be loveable and to be enough.

I didn't have to prove to God that I was okay. I didn't have to be accomplishing all of these things in life to be loved by God. I literally feel a weight lift from my shoulders, and I smile as it floats off of my back. I smile on the inside and sip on the last drop of green tea. I feel like I just found the key— my magic key to understanding my life. I had carried that invisible weight for a very long time, and now it's time for it to be gone. I don't need it anymore for the new life that I'm creating. It's become crystal clear that my new purpose is to trust God fully and completely with all areas of my life. I mean gosh, I had already literally placed my life in His hands, and He didn't mess that up, right?

June 2009

I continue to review my life and realize that I've accomplished so much in my 30-plus years on the planet and that I've been blessed in lots of ways—many graduations, varied work experiences, great relationships (well, they weren't all great), amazing family and friends. On top of all this, I've traveled, and I've started a couple of businesses. I can't help but think that I was really on the right path in my life. Spiritually, I had grown so much over the past five years. I lived a good life, and I treated people with Love. I feel the anger coming back.

God, why did You let this happen to me? I think that I'll never understand why bad things happen to good people. In moments like this, I'm so angry that I can't even talk to God anymore. I'm angry with God. And if you're wondering whether or not it's okay to be mad at God, well it is. God can take it. But I soon realize that I can't possibly be with angry with God forever because He's the one who has gotten me through this mess.

My big realization after looking through a snapshot of my life is that there has to be something more than what I'm living for. I've done all the things you're "supposed" to do in your 20s and early 30s. Where do I go from here? I look at the list of questions I wrote down about this whole experience, and I still don't have answers. So many people around me comment on how brave I am, but I don't feel brave. I feel confused. I would have never guessed in a million years that this could happen to me. I mean, isn't there an easier way to show how brave you are?

I don't know if I have the strength to keep going. The smallest things like getting out of bed require so much effort. I'm not at all excited about starting over. I really liked my life before all of this happened. I have survived being shot; I have no money, no job; I have moved back in with my parents, and I have no idea what to do next. This isn't the ideal way to start over in life. People keep telling me that I'll get clarity soon. But right now? This just SUCKS. Really, really SUCKS.

I'm beginning to see a pattern to my deep sadness. On the first day, I'm deeply sad—so sad that I can't even cry. I don't think that crying will help or change things, but I can definitely tell that my body is crying. My heart feels heavy with grief, like it's just going to fall out of my body. My voice, which is usually upbeat, has a deeper tone, weighed down with sadness; it's heavy. I move slowly because I feel so much intense, emotional pain. Then I start to write—a lot. I get my journal out and just write off and on all day. If I'm not writing, I'm sleeping. I feel hopeless—beyond confused and overwhelmed.

I wake up later than normal on the second day of sadness, just kind of in a daze, pinching myself as if I'm trying to wake up from a nightmare. Then I grab my cell phone to call one of my closest friends. For some reason, I need to talk and vent with a family member or friend before I let out a big cry. Once I begin talking to someone, I start to feel that tingling in my throat, and I hear that murmur in my voice as it gets weak and shaky until mid-sentence I blurt out something like, "I C-A-N-T believe that this happened to me! Why did God do this to me?" I can hardly get the words out without huffing and puffing like a little kid, and I can hear how sad my spirit sounds. And then, it's the flood of tears—like a weak dam has been holding back the tears for centuries and when that dam breaks, all the tears come rushing out. If the tears could talk, they would probably thank me for setting them free.

Thank God for my friend Yvonne. She's one of the very few friends I feel safe enough with to call and just tell her that I need to cry—and she'll just listen and let me feel safe. When I'm done, she always provides something inspirational. She helps me realize that there is a purpose for all of this. After the crying spell, I feel a mix of emotions. I feel lighter and my heart feels like it's smiling, but I've done so much releasing that I need to go to sleep and recharge.

By the third day I feel a lot better, but I still take it easy with myself. I still move very slowly. If I watch TV, it's something light-hearted and funny. By the fourth day, I feel much more stable, so I do something active like go for a walk or hang out with friends.

Usually somewhere between that third or fourth day, I start to get some kind of sign from God that I'm not broken. I hear God's voice tell me that everything is going to be okay. I'm learning that God speaks to me a lot through inspiration—out of nowhere, I'll get an idea to do something. For instance, today I decided to go and register for a Spanish class. I took Spanish in high school, and I took a year of it in college, but I'm not fluent yet. It's a goal that I've had for a really long time, and now I'm ready to work toward my goal. So, that's what I did—I drove to a language school and signed up for a class. Then I caught up with some friends who I really enjoy talking to. I just woke up this morning and decided I wanted to have a good day. I chose to focus on creating a good day instead of worrying about my list of life questions that I don't have answers to or agonizing about my future or about money.

I'm learning that I can't take on the whole world at once. I have to take everything in small bites. I have to live for now. The whole idea of being in the moment has really taken on new meaning for me, so I deal with today and with this moment that I know I have. In these moments when I really KNOW that the moment is all I have, I don't even worry about my problems. I can't live in the now and be worried about the past or the future at the same time.

My new outlook on goals is this: Having goals, plans, and visions for your life is great. It's good and necessary to have an idea of what you want to accomplish in life. Goals keep you excited about life, but we have to realize that life is always changing and evolving and so are we. So instead of being ATTACHED to our goals, we need to give them the freedom to evolve and change.

I think back to when I was 21years old and working at my college internship. I remember I whipped out a piece of paper and started writing out my timeline for the next 10 years. The 31-year-old me seemed so far away. The funniest thing is that I realized very few of those goals my 21-year-old self had set. As I got older, a lot of the things that I desired changed. For example, by the time I was 25, I really wasn't ready to be married and have my first child by the time I was 26 (as I thought I would when I was 21). When I turned 26, I was just enjoying life and having fun.

I'm somewhat excited to go back to my home in Maryland even though I know for sure that I'm definitely not living in that house again. The plan is to be in Maryland for eight days and move all of my stuff out of the house. I've also made appointments with doctors for checkups to make sure I'm healing okay. My father is making the cross-country trip with me, and my youngest brother, Eric, is flying in from his college in Minnesota.

I have mixed emotions right now. I'm happy to go back and see my friends, but I really just want the moving process to happen as quickly as possible. I've been getting so much rest in California, and now it's time for the big move. A mild depression sets in days before the trip. I feel overwhelmed. There is a deep and heavy sadness in my spirit and my body feels heavy, like I'm walking around with a ton of bricks on my back. When I have these low points, I just feel like I'm living for other people. I'm numb—not really excited to be alive, and not really ready to leave.

My father and I talk a lot about everything that's happened this year. We've always been close, but this experience has brought us even closer. On my sad days, he reminds me that it's going to be like this for a while—I'll have a few bad days then a good day, but one day there will be lots more good days than bad days. I love that my parents allow me to grieve and go through this process in a very safe place. I feel so vulnerable now, but I'm surrounded by so much love that it makes it easier to get through it all.

The flight from the West Coast to the East Coast is a long one, taking about five or six hours. I love flying—I always have. It reminds me of the adventure of life. I like listening to my iPod and reading my magazines. I have to confess, the only time I ever buy the gossip magazines is when I fly. I don't know how or when it became part of my flying ritual, but I always buy a fashion magazine, an inspirational magazine, and one or sometimes two of the Hollywood gossip magazines. I think the gossip magazines are just something juicy to read to help those hours go by faster.

On the flight, my dad and I review all the things we need to do in Maryland. I'm so glad that my brother, Eric is meeting us because it's clear that we have our work cut out for us. I'm so anxious on the flight that I don't even take a nap. I feel chatty, but my dad sleeps most of the flight so I just entertain myself. When we land in Maryland, we collect our luggage and wait for my brother to arrive about an hour later.

As soon as we walk outside to our ride, I feel the thick, muggy humidity of the East Coast—a constant reminder that summer is here. The ride from the airport to my house is about fifteen minutes. When we pull up to my house, I get an immediate knot in my stomach—the same uneasiness and nervousness I felt on the evening of January 14th. I feel like I'm going to be sick. I sit in the car and take a minute for myself as my father, brother, and friend unload the luggage from the car.

In a flash of maybe five seconds or less, I see the whole shooting scenario flash in front of my eyes. I see it as if I'm watching a movie. I want to yell to myself, "RUN, RUN, RUN! He's got a gun!" And then I see myself fall and hit the ground, and I see him running away. Then I take a breath and realize that it's June, not January, and that I'm definitely safe in this moment.

I kind of snap out of the movie and look up at my father,

brother, and friend, who are standing at the top of the stairs waiting for me to unlock the door. I can tell that they realize I'm having a moment. Then, without a word from me, my brother runs down the stairs to the car.

"Soyini? You okay?" He watches my face. "Dad said you don't have to get out if you're not ready. We can just come back tomorrow if you aren't comfortable."

"No," I say, "I'm okay?" I hear the question mark in my voice. Am I okay? I think to myself. Can I really do this right now? Before I answer the question, I jump out of the car and start walking up the stairs to the front door of my house. When I get to the door, my dad hugs me and tells me he's proud of me. As I unlock the door, I turn around and realize that the moment I chose not to unlock the front door in January is part of the reason I'm still here in June.

We walk in the house and it's just the way I left it a few months ago. The windows haven't been opened in a while, so it's warm and stuffy and smells stale. We put the luggage down on the living room floor, and I immediately walk through all the rooms of my house as if it's an old friend whom I haven't seen in a while. I remember how safe I always felt in my home and how much I enjoyed entertaining and having friends over. I enjoyed decorating my home—it took me about a year to make it look like I really wanted it to.

As I walk through each room, I survey how much I've collected in the past four years. I feel proud because this is my first home, which I actually purchased on my own. I was so proud the day I went to closing—it was a strong sense of accomplishment. As I walk through the kitchen, I remember cooking a nice home-cooked meal for my birthday and having some of my closest friends come by and celebrate with me. We ate, drank wine, watched movies, and laughed. As I exit the kitchen and walk to the living room, I can still hear my friends' and my laughter from various get-togethers and parties that I've had over the years. I have so many fond memories of my home.

I walk upstairs and sit in my office/prayer room for a while. The walls are beautiful. I painted them a rich violet color, and everything else in the room is cream or white. It's just such a beautiful space. It was the most peaceful room in the house— I purposely designed it that way. I sit on the carpet and just take it all in for a moment. Out of nowhere, a tear runs down my cheek, and then another one, and another. It hits me that I'm here to pack up my house. I have to move. I've enjoyed living here, but my life has changed dramatically, and I have a little over a week to pack everything up. I'm shipping my life back to the West Coast, and I just need a moment to take it all in. I stretch out on the cream-colored carpet and silently sob until my dad and brother walk up the stairs to tell me that we should all go and grab something to eat.

For a couple reasons, our planned, one-week trip to Maryland to move my stuff has turned into a month-long stay. Several doctors' appointments have stretched my time out further and further, as has preparing my home to move. I've always hated moving. It seems like it takes forever, and you never realize how much stuff you have until you start trying to box it up. Moving back to the West Coast means I'll have much less space, so my biggest question is, "How will I get a house full of stuff to fit in one bedroom at my parents' home?"

This trip to Maryland is filled with so much clean-up: doctors' visits, paperwork, bills, and quick visits with friends in between moving.

I even manage to squeeze in some time to share my story with a group at my church, but going back to my church was surreal as it was literally the last place I visited before my life changed forever.

When I walk into the church, I feel a chill. I walk into the classroom where I took a class on the evening of January 14th and sit down in the same space that I sat that night five months ago. I can still remember how nervous I felt that night—very distracted and unsettled on the inside with no clue about what was coming that fateful night. Unlike that night in January, today I'm not alone.

My dad stayed home to finish packing and moving things, but my brother is with me. Although I'm tired, I decide to honor my commitment to my church and speak. I'm wearing one of my favorite sundresses that's splashed with orange, chocolate, and white in the print. I chose this dress because orange is one of my favorite colors—it makes me feel so energized.

As I walk into the sanctuary, I hold my brother's hand and follow the pastor to the podium. I was expecting to talk to a small group of 15 or so; however, there are probably 60 to 70 people present. I'm nervous, and my palms are sweaty. What am I going to tell everyone? Will I be able to make it through my talk without crying uncontrollably? Maybe I shouldn't do this. Maybe I'm not ready to speak. I've begun to notice that at the moment when I'm about to do what God is calling me to do, fear steps in and causes me to doubt myself and what I need to do. That's what those insecure thoughts represent. In this moment, I can choose to give into fear, but I decide that what I have to say is important. So, I take a deep breath and look at the notes that I scribbled down on a piece of paper on the way to the church.

As I stand up, I take a moment to look around the room at all of the smiling, loving faces. I see men and women, young and old, and I know that the people in this space love me and are happy to know that I'm alive. So in that moment, I trust myself and God, and I speak from my heart. The more I speak, the deeper I come to understand how important our testimonies are to others. When I finish, almost everyone comes up and talks to me about how my story has inspired and encouraged them. I know that I've done what I was supposed to do. When I look over at my brother, he's just smiling and happy—I can see that he's so proud to see me share.

There hasn't been one empty moment since we've been back in Maryland. If I'm not at a doctor's appointment, we are moving, painting, cleaning—you name it. It overwhelms me at times, but I know that we have work to do. As we clean, I go through so many clothes and shoes that I no longer need, so I take them to the Salvation Army. We also decide to have a yard sale so that I can get rid of some of my large items like the TV and couch. Every time I give away or sell something, I feel one chapter of my life ending and another one beginning. I'm selling items for less than half of what I paid for them, but we're working with such a tight time frame that I have no choice except to almost give items away.

Today is my last surgery, and it's a minor one: I've been walking around with bullet fragments in my jaw. I don't really feel them, but they're in there, and it makes me sad when I think about those fragments being in my jaw. Although I had several surgeries in January, I'm nervous about getting the fragments removed because I have no memory of those other operations. I remind myself that it should be a simple surgery in my doctor's office and that I have no reason to worry.

My dad and my brother accompany me to the doctor's office. The entire time, I'm just praying that everything works out fine. If God got me this far, then I know that He will keep me here. Dr. Le and his two assistants greet me in his office.

Dr. Le is very meticulous and takes his time to explain things well. After he describes the procedure to me, he asks if I have any questions. My only concern is pain.

Ironically, I'm certain that my tolerance for pain has increased this year, so it's funny that I'm worried about it at all. I've had needles injected into every part of my body. I've had blood drawn so many times. Every part of me has been nicked, plucked, and pinched. So yes, my fear of pain is much less than it used to be. Plus, one of the gifts that a very spiritual friend of mine gave me is a rose quartz stone. It's beautiful, and it's supposed to help me relieve stress—I just need to hold it to remain calm and focus on my breathing. I'm not sure if this really works, but I'm willing to try it today.

At first the doctor puts some numbing cream on my jaw and I sit in the chair, giving it some time to do its thing. After about a half hour or so, Dr. Le and his assistants come in. I see the needle and all his other tools sitting on the table next to me. I just try to focus on other things like hanging out with friends or thinking about my future—anything that I can think of to get my mind off of what is about to happen. One of Dr. Le's assistants, who I believe is in medical school or working on his residency, can tell that I'm a little nervous, so he makes some small talk with me. I don't normally like small talk, but in this moment, I really appreciate it. Okay, they're ready to go.

First, I think he drains some of the excess pus that's in my jaw, and then I can feel him tugging on my jaw as if he's made an opening in my skin. They all tell me to relax and that I'm doing a great job. I have my eyes closed the entire time so that I can maintain my relaxed state. It seems like I'm in there forever, but it probably took only about an hour. Then I hear one of the assistants say something like, "Oh, wow, look at it," and I hear something make a thumping sound as it hits a tray. I can tell it's a piece of the fragment. I guess it's one of the bigger pieces. A few moments later, I hear Dr. Le say that he's going to stitch me up, and I can feel a single tear run down the left side of my face. I'm relieved that it's over, but I'm so tired of this whole process. I've never had to visit doctors this much in my entire life.

Before I leave, Dr. Le applies the head dressing to make sure that my wound heals properly. He shows my dad, brother, and me how to apply the head dressing and gives us instructions on how to maintain it until my follow-up visit the next week. The head dressing is very uncomfortable—it just feels weird to have an Ace bandage wrapped around your head for a week. But, I tell myself that this is just something that I have to do for the healing process. When I arrive home, my dad informs me that Michael Jackson has died. The sadness of Michael's death hurt me to the core, I had no more thoughts that night about what I was going through. Michael was always my favorite singer, and his music formed the soundtrack of my adolescent life.

In the week before my follow-up visit to Dr. Le, my house has turned into a yard sale. Every day, people are coming in to check out my couch, dishes, bed, TV, bedroom furniture— everything. I'm still wearing the head gear while this is going on—I even go to the grocery store and the movies and run errands with this head gear on. This process has made me so empathic with people with disabilities. People stare at me and give me this look like, "What happened to you?"

I remember in the beginning, when I had to wear a patch over my eye, I was at the grocery store with my mother when a child (who looked to be about 10 years old) pointed directly at me and yelled out, "Mommy, look at the pirate lady." I kind of laughed to myself and felt embarrassed at the same time. Then there was the time when I was at the gas station and a strange man walked up to me, looking as if he wanted to cry for me, and said, "I'm going to go home and pray for you." He said it with so much pity in his voice—and I didn't need or want his pity. I'm extra careful now not to stare at someone who looks different because I've learned there is always a story behind the wounds or the bruises. When I see people now who have disabilities or physical deformities, I look beyond their physical appearance and see their inner beauty.

My father and I vacuumed the floors for the last time, and we've done our final walk-through of my house. We're both exhausted. I can see it in my dad when I look at him. His eyes are a little red and he has small bags under his eyes. We both need a long nap. I'm so thankful that he and my brother were able to help me; I couldn't have done it without them.

We were up daily at 6:30 a.m., cleaning and moving furniture around all day long. I was never in bed before one or two every morning. It seemed like we would never finish, and there were so many days that I just didn't feel like doing anything. All I wanted to do was just lie in bed and cry all day long because I knew that I was going to be starting over. The road ahead of me seemed so long.

I was also tired because of all the memories I relived, driving around in my neighborhood. I would always pass a place or see something that reminded me of "him." Sometimes I'd see a car similar to his and my heart would almost jump out of my chest. These were all memories that I wanted to forget, and they wore me out.

Finally, almost a month after we arrived, we can leave Maryland. At this point I'm so ready to get out of here. I sold all of the major items during my yard sale, but I gave away and threw away so much more than I sold. I just look at it as if I'm giving a gift to the universe, and I know that it will all come back to me. Moving has been a big energy release, though, and I feel so drained. Moving away from Maryland is like moving away from a nightmare. I still can't believe how much happened on that January night.

With the last cleaning tasks complete, we've finished everything, and the house feels peaceful. It's empty and quiet. The only thing left in my house is carpet and bare walls. My dad and I sit on the floor in the middle of the dining room, waiting for our ride to the airport. I can't believe how much we accomplished in one month's time. I hear our ride outside, honking the horn. My dad and I slowly stand up, grab our bags, and walk out to the car.

I'm still so overwhelmed with thoughts of the new life I have to build. I don't think any of us are ever ready to make such a sudden change, but when life changes so quickly, we have to change too. I'm also still hurt because there is no justice for the way that he violated me: I almost lost my life, endured countless surgeries, am haunted by memories and nightmares, have been emotionally traumatized, incurred massive debt, and I've had to change my life overnight. I really hate "him" right now. I know that I didn't deserve any of this.

What keeps me going is that brighter days have to be ahead of me because I've been living the darkest days of my life for the past five months. Then I realize that I can't keep hating him because we're just "souls inside of a body." He no longer exists. His body is under the ground decaying and his soul is somewhere else. His soul is on a journey on some other plane that we don't know about on Earth. I know that he had to be experiencing a lot of inner turmoil to do what he did. There was probably pain inside of him that I will never know or understand. So, I remind myself that I need to let these thoughts go, and I fall into a deep sleep beside my father as I listen to the plane's engines hum. I don't even wake up for the complimentary peanuts and beverage.

As soon as our flight lands in the San Francisco Bay area, I feel a huge amount of relief. It's been such a long road. Instinctively I know that my arrival means the beginning of a brand new chapter in my life, so I take a moment to reflect on all of the things that I did in my nine years on the East Coast as I really did enjoy my life and my career. I made friends that I will have for the rest of my life. I traveled all around the world. I dated some of the most interesting and fun men that I have ever known. My life on the East Coast was many things, but it was never boring. Although I love my family dearly, I really enjoyed being so far away and creating my own life. As strange as it sounds, I don't have any regrets for any decisions that I made. Every decision has caused me to be exactly where I am. At each moment or stage in my life, I made the best decision that I could make in the moment.

I don't know if it's the laidback culture of the West Coast or what, but I feel so much lighter here. The pace is definitely slower. The people are a little more kind. The weather, of course, is beautiful. And I don't feel like I am rushing to do anything in particular. Before January 14, 2009, I was always trying to make something happen. Now I know that I can just live for a while. I still have absolutely no idea what I'm going to do going forward. My life is still an empty canvas, and I'm intimidated by all that I have to do.

As my father and I walk out of the airport to wait for my mother to pick us up, I just take in the scenery—the beautiful, clear blue sky, the emerald green trees, and the warm air. As I take a deep breath, I realize that there is no humidity—I can tell that I'm definitely back home on the West Coast.

When we get home, my mother and some other family members have a huge dinner prepared for us. It always feels good to have a nice home-cooked meal after a long flight across the country. We all eat, talk, laugh, and eat again. After the long day, I'm exhausted and I go to bed.

At 4:04 a.m., I pop up out of a deep sleep. I notice that whenever God wants my attention, he wakes me up at the craziest times in the morning, like 3:18 a.m. or 5:02 a.m. It's always an early, random time and I feel like God is saying to me, "You're late for our appointment" because I pop up so suddenly and feel rushed like I'm late for an important meeting or something. I can never get back to sleep after this sudden interruption. I usually lie in bed and allow all the thoughts of what I need to do run through my mind, or I pick up my journal and start writing. However, on this Friday morning at 4:04 a.m. Pacific Standard Time, I just have the realization of where I am.

I sit up in bed, and the first thing I realize is that it's not my soft, cushy pillow-top mattress from Maryland. Then I reach over to the night stand on my left and turn on the lamp. I look around the room and I don't see my bedroom furniture. And then it hits me—this is my new home for the next few … months? Maybe years? I'm not in Maryland anymore. I'm 3,000 miles away in my parents' home, and I'm overcome with sadness.

I feel the void that's left after everything has been stripped away from me so quickly and unexpectedly. I lost my home, my furniture, most of my savings, and my old self. My head spins as I think about all that I lost in such a short period of time. I just sit up in bed and quietly sob, mourning again for the life that I lost. I feel that deep sadness—almost a hollowness—in my soul. I have no plan for how I am going to change my situation; I just know that I am beyond overwhelmed and I need help.

Why would God allow me to suffer so much? To survive an attempted homicide is already a lot. To lose a body part is also very overwhelming. But then to also realize that God kept me here for a reason that I presently don't understand is beyond overwhelming. I can honestly say, "God, I don't understand you at all. Why me? What do you want from me?" I actually say these words out loud to God as if He is sitting at the foot of the bed looking at me.

I look on the night stand again and notice a box of tissues, so I grab a few and continue to ask the same two questions over and over again. My disbelief that I've actually endured two gunshot wounds and am alive to even question what happened to me never diminishes. I keep seeing flashbacks of that night. I see myself doing all of my normal activities that day. I feel the discomfort of my spirit telling me that something is wrong. I keep hearing the last words that he said to me. I see him pull out the gun in slow motion. This all just doesn't make sense. I'm angry that I have to feel such pain. I continue to cry and ask God questions all night, but there is SILENCE. Mind-numbing SILENCE. I wake up at 10 a.m. with puffy eyes and wadded tissues in my hand. I feel a little lighter, but God is still silent.

There are a few good things about being at my parents' house. I have all the love and support that I need from them, and I still have lots of childhood friends here—friends whom I've known since kindergarten. It's always good to have people in your life who know the real you. These are friends that I walked to school with. We watched cartoons at each other's house. We rode bikes and played tag until the sun came down. As a child, that's how I knew dinner was ready. I had a really good childhood—just long, carefree days where all I had to do was be a kid. Life was fun. Wow, life was so simple back then.

So today, some of my friends from the neighborhood and I are getting together for brunch. We all meet up at my house. One by one, they come in and we give each other a big hug. They each have a look of relief in their eyes after seeing for themselves that I'm alive and look so normal. I think that none of them knew what to expect.

There are lots of tears and hugs and some quick catching up before we go to brunch. I haven't seen a few of them in more than ten years, but there is something about childhood connections that makes it so that time and distance don't matter. We all look the same, just grown up. I can still see us as ten-year-old little girls running around the neighborhood, being chased by the boys, and playing with dolls.

It's like a mini reunion in my house as we swap stories: "Remember that summer from sixth grade when …?" Or "I wonder what happened to … who used to hang with us in eighth grade." It's as if we're having an unofficial contest to see who can recount the best childhood memory. I'm so happy to see my friends. Family and friends always energize me.

When we get to the restaurant, we continue to catch up on stories. And then it hits me—this experience of being back home is like therapy. It reminds me that my life is more than just the events that took place the night of January 14, 2009. That night is definitely part of my story, but it's a chapter in my story, not my entire story. I'm reminded that I had a happy life before all of this happened, and I will continue to have a happy life going forward.

The chatting and the laughing at the table stop for a moment. I'm sitting in between two of my friends, and the friends directly in front of me and on both sides of me are all kind of looking at me. As if they want to say something. I can tell that my friend Janine, sitting directly in front of me, is about to speak. Janine is one of my friends who came out of the womb as an adult. She has always been mature. In fact, one of my best memories of her is when we were about eight years old, we were all playing outside, and she looked to me and another friend and said, "You guys are so childish." I will never forget that moment. (I'm laughing as I write this now.) But it was a moment that I'll never forget that truly captures how mature she's always been. Now as a wife and mother, she has that same seriousness whenever she speaks. So she asks me, "How are you doing?"

I know that we've all kind of been avoiding this question, but it's definitely something that needs to be discussed. It's just that I never really know how to start answering it because I don't always know how I'm doing. Most days, I feel so conflicted: I'm thankful to be alive but sometimes I'm just angry with God for allowing this to happen. But then I realize that my friends really want to know what's happened. All they know is that we hadn't talked in a really long time, and then they got the news about the shooting. When I step outside of myself and I think about things from a different perspective, I can only imagine how difficult it is to hear that someone you care about and have known for so long is going through such a great tragedy. So I decide to open up.

I give them all the background on how the relationship started and how it turned really bad. The entire time I'm speaking, no one touches their food or drinks their juice. All eyes are on me. They are all so focused on every detail. I can see each one of their faces showing the full range of emotion that they're feeling on the inside. I also sense that each one of them is getting from my experience what they needed to learn, and that's when it hits me—sometimes a "good person" will endure something really bad so that the people around them can learn a few lessons.

I know that I've had countless friends share my story with some of their friends. I've also seen how some of my friends have learned from my experience and decided to make overdue choices and decisions. After I've finished sharing my story, we all kind of take a deep breath and order another round of mimosas.

It's really hard when things fall apart. The process of recovering is so difficult. Although this tragedy almost ended my life, life hasn't stopped. I still have the pressure of keeping up with bills even though my income has dwindled down to almost nothing. My life is far from normal right now. As a matter of fact, it's a mess. But I have come to embrace the fact that it's my own mess. And I acknowledge the fact that it's going to take a while to get it all back on track.

Moving back west was a huge milestone for me. Up until this point, I haven't had a chance to really rest. There were constant appointments to handle and business to take care of while I was in Maryland. I didn't have long moments to reflect because I was always on the go. As hard as it is to believe, I haven't stopped moving. I feel like I'm always juggling ideas of my past, present, and future—retracing moments of my life with him , scrutinizing details and possible warning signs from the past, crying and grieving about the present and confused about the future. It's just so much at once.

The timing of my move back to California is actually good. Somehow it turns out that my entire family is there all at once. My brothers and I are at various turning points, and we've come home to build our new lives. When I was on the East Coast, I lived by myself for a long time, and I was so used to making it on my own. When I needed to feel connected to my family, I would call. I especially looked forward to the holidays when we would be together for about two weeks. I always felt so energized afterwards. For about ten years, I was used to seeing everyone for two weeks, and then it was off to Maryland to live my own life.

Honestly though, over the last few years, I was getting a little tired of being away from my family. As I got older, I realized that family is really all you have in life. You only get one family, and you can't get back any missed time with them. In the back of my mind, I always knew that I would return home at some point, but I never imagined I'd do it under such drastic circumstances.

My mother reminds me that while I'm at home, the only thing I need to worry about is getting settled here and resting.

"Just relax, sweetheart," she tells me. "You've been through so much, just take it easy. Don't even think about what you're going to do next, just let it come to you."

My mother is a very serious person. She's extremely introspective and an analyzer of life, a teacher, and the sweetest person I know. My father is an entrepreneur who loves his family. He's from the South and is a very laidback, carefree person who enjoys being alive. He comes up with these little "country sayings" that get right to the point of some serious life questions that I have. Through his actions, he reminds me of the simplicity of life.

Whenever I talk to my parents, I understand my personality so much; I see myself in both of them. When I look at them, I know that I couldn't get through any of this mess without them. They let me cry when I need to cry, they let me talk to them for hours about the same memories over and over again, and they let me ramble on about how confused I am about all the changes and adjustments that I continue to make. My mom and dad have been the same constant loving force in my life no matter what I've ever gone through in my life. For that, I am eternally grateful to have them as parents.

My brothers and I have been hanging out too. We go to the movies and out to eat every week. It gives me something to look forward to, and it gives us a chance to bond again. We laugh a lot and talk a lot about childhood memories or about life. The time with them also takes my mind off of everything that has happened.

As I've said before, my time was always occupied before January 14, 2009. I was working as a sales professional, going to the gym, traveling, spending time with friends, dating, going to church—a full life. A life that I enjoyed. I always had something to do. When I had free moments, I felt a little guilty. I think that this is all part of the Western culture—we are so busy doing that we never have a chance to Just Be in life. Life happens in the moment, but we're already in the future or stuck in the past. Most of us feel like we always need to be accomplishing something. The problem that I've come to see with this way of life is that we never have time to be still. I've gone to different spiritual workshops in the past and read books about "being in the moment" or "sitting still." I understood it intellectually, but I don't think that I understood that idea on an emotional or spiritual level. Little did I know that all of that would start to change once I moved to California.

My days start a whole lot later in California. I wake up late because I sometimes have nightmares in the middle of the night and can't get back to sleep. I also just need a lot more rest these days, so I wake up later in the morning. If I'm hungry, I have a little breakfast, then I spend a little time writing in my journal. The highlight of my day is getting out for some quiet time to take a walk and be in nature.

Being outside, especially near water, helps me relax. As I walk, I listen to my favorite music or an inspirational podcast that I've saved on my iPod. As I walk past people, I can't believe that I'm still alive. I usually just stop at some point during my walk and give thanks to God for keeping me here. I have learned to let the bad memories of what happened come and go. If I fight the memories, they just come back stronger. So I just let them come and flow out like the ocean.

Then one day, it occurred to me to just say my Forgiveness statements out loud. So when I get to the point where I'm hating him really bad, where I can feel the hate build up in my heart, I just forgive him. I say it out loud a few times until I really feel it and believe it in my heart. This isn't easy—trust me. But I know that if I hold it all in, I'll probably get sick.

I have also learned to ask God for exactly what I need in the moment. Sometimes people get so caught up in the right way to pray or the right way to talk to God. This experience has humbled me so much that I just have a different perspective on things. When I go to God with a pure heart and sincerely ask for what I need in that moment, my prayers are always answered. For the most part, I ask for Grace, Mercy, and Peace. It works for me. I'll leave religion for everyone else.

As I get to know God, I see that I'm building a relationship of my very own with Him. There is no right or wrong way, there is just Love. These daily walks have become my scheduled appointment with God, and this time in nature restores me. I talk to God, ask questions, pray for wisdom, and then I just get quiet. For months now, people have been telling me that my story and my testimony are going to help people. On this day sitting at the marina, looking at the waves flow and listening to the peacefulness of nature, I get a strong feeling deep down in my spirit that confirms my assignment. God speaks to me very clearly and lets me know that I'm ready to live this purpose.

Once a week, I also talk to my therapist. It's great to have family and friends to talk to, but I don't want to wear them out with the heaviness of this experience. So my therapist is also part of my support team. She helps me process my experience and uncover new insights.

July 2009

I've made it to my six-month mark. Every time there is a significant milestone like this, I talk to my family and close friends about it. We celebrate the fact that I'm alive and well. And I celebrate the fact that this experience hasn't broken me. I have definitely been shattered, but I'm not broken.

I still have days when I struggle to have faith when nothing seems to change. My savings is dwindling down rapidly, I'm going through all kinds of changes, bill collectors are calling me, and I'm still undecided about tomorrow. Even with all of these things to worry about, I feel an inner protection happening inside of me. I'll have moments where I feel really down and depressed, but I can go only so low. Inevitably, something will snap me out of it. I am determined not to let this experience ruin me.

Every day I ask God to give me wisdom and allow me to see this experience clearly. It's a slow, gradual process, but I can feel the insights coming. Today I have the strong awareness that I'm free to begin creating a new life. My life is no longer about achieving for the sake of achieving. My new life will be lived with meaning and purpose.

As I'm taking my daily walk today, I decide to go back to school to get my MBA. This idea just comes to me from out of nowhere. I haven't even been thinking about what I need to do next—it just comes to me, as a very natural process. I like this whole idea of letting life come to you. I guess this is what my parents have been telling me.

This is definitely one of the lowest points in my life. I can't wrap my head around it. It doesn't make any sense. I've worked really hard my entire life and all I have to show for it is $100 in the bank. I've been living on my savings for the past several months. Now, I only have $100 in there. I literally feel like the air has been knocked out of me.

Every time I think that I have lifted myself up and escaped a deep depression, something like this happens to knock me back down. I'm overwhelmed and absolutely frustrated today. I'm having one of those moments where I'm angry with God and want to know why He is allowing all of this suffering. I want to ask God, "Where are you?" On days like this, when it gets really bad, I just give up. I know that I've done everything in my power to prevent any of this from happening, and now I realize there's nothing else I can do. I have to find it in myself to trust that everything will be all right. I have no idea when or how, but tomorrow has to be a better day.

My parents keep telling me that God wouldn't bring me this far and just drop me. "He has a plan for your life," my mother tells me. Her deep brown eyes are tired and full of concern. Her usually soft voice sounds almost like a whisper. As she always does, she asks me, "What can I do to make this better for you?"

My mother is hurting as much as I am. It's difficult for a parent to see their child suffer—especially because my parents know that I was always a good kid and grew up to be a very responsible and loving adult. I can hear in my mother's voice that she is also questioning God and trying to make sense of all of this. I haven't rested since January 14, and neither has she.

I can remember when I was in the hospital waiting for my parents to come visit me. I had tubes down my throat so I couldn't talk and I had bandages all around my head. My eye was covered up too. I had to communicate by nodding my head yes and shaking it no. When I was excited to see someone, I would simply grab their hand.

I was sleeping when my parents first entered my hospital room. I remember waking up and they were in front of me. At first, I thought that I was dreaming. My mother grabbed my right hand, and my hands were so swollen from all of the pain medication that I couldn't even clench my fist. Because I couldn't squeeze her hand, she just stroked my hand and told me, "Everything's going to be okay. Just relax, honey. Mom and Dad are here."

My complexion was extremely pale from the loss of blood, and I was told later that my entire body was so swollen that I didn't look like myself. When my parents first saw me, I later found out that they said, "That's not our daughter." I looked so different that my own parents didn't recognize me.

Now, several months later, my mother has flashbacks of the first time she saw me in the hospital. Sometimes when we're sitting on the couch watching TV, she'll look at me, grab my hand, and say, "I still remember when you couldn't grab my hand." Moments like that deeply affect me. I can see how much this has hurt my mother. On one particular July afternoon she grabbed my hand and said something like, "I wish I could have done something to protect you. I wish you didn't have to suffer like this."

Mom often tells me that she and my father don't know what they would do without me—I'm the oldest child and their only daughter. When I was in critical condition in the hospital, the doctor called my parents to tell them what happened. My mother screamed and fell on the floor. My father told me that she kept saying, "I can't live without my baby." My father was in complete shock too. At that point no one knew whether or not I would make it. Only God knew my fate.

To this day, I tear up every time I think about my parents getting that initial call. They were 3,000 miles away from me when they found out that I had been shot and might not be alive by the time they got to Maryland. The thought of what they went through sends chills down my spine. I'm just thankful that God has kept me here to be with them. When I think about these memories, I can see that my most difficult days are behind me.

After several sad days following my discovery that I have only $100 in the bank , I decide that I don't want to keep living like this. I've been sitting in my room with a box of tissues, crying all day. I write in my journal too—letters to God asking why I needed to go through this horrible experience. A different family member comes into my room every so often to check on me. They're so concerned, but I've been so depressed that I can't even talk. Every time I attempt to talk, I cry. When I look in the mirror, I see how sad and depressed I look.

I do think I needed this time to be alone in my room to sort things out by myself. The grieving process is very natural, and I needed to be alone with my own thoughts to heal. When I'm around my family and friends, I try to keep an upbeat spirit so that they feel better. But the truth is I was really hurting. I was questioning life and God. In my darkest moments, there were times when I really questioned whether I wanted to go on living. I was questioning everything that I had ever believed about God. I was angry with Him. And I was angry with and hating the person that did this to me. I was searching for answers. I felt like my soul had turned upside down.

Even though I'm still getting over my depression, some-where in my spirit I know that I have two choices: 1) I can stay in that bedroom and cry for the rest of my life; or 2) I can get on with my life and take one day at a time. After all, I want to see how this whole thing turns out!

I have the idea to start researching grad schools in my area. I also begin looking into writer's workshops, and I register for a one-day writer's workshop in San Francisco. Dwayne volunteers to drive me to the workshop, and the drive to San Francisco is beautiful. I really do see why people around the world love the beauty of the San Francisco Bay Area. You can't beat the weather, and the Bay Area is one of the most scenic places I've ever been.

Even with the beautiful surroundings, I'm quiet on the drive to the workshop with my brother—fighting back the tears. I'm battling thoughts filled with doubt and fear about being around strangers. My brother tries so hard to pull conversa-tion from me, asking me questions about the workshop, etc. But my silence lets him know that I'm not in the mood to talk. I've got a roller coaster of emotions going on inside of me, and I'm nervous about spending a full day with a bunch of strangers. All year, I've carefully selected my contact with new people. I always have a family member or friend with me, and we usually go someplace where I feel really comfort-able. I've kind of insulated myself from the outside world.

As we drive up one of San Francisco's hilly streets, I feel like I'm on a roller coaster—you know the feeling—the roller coaster goes straight up a very steep track just before it makes the inevitable powerful drop. Well that's what this hill is like. The workshop is being held in this beautiful Victorian home.

I'm about ten minutes late, so the instructor calls me on my cell phone, and I tell her that I'll be there in five minutes. In reality, I'm sitting in the car in front of the place, crying and telling my brother that I don't know if I can do this. I don't know if I can pull myself together and go in with a bunch of strangers.

My brother tells me that we can go home if I want to, that he'll just go tell the instructor we had a change of plans. He tells me there's no pressure or rush for me to do anything I don't want to do. I'm staring out the window looking at the beautiful San Francisco Bay Area, and I think to myself, "I want to experience life again." I don't want to spend another day crying and lying around. I take a few more minutes in the car to wipe away the tears then I tell my brother that I want to go, but I add, "Stay in the area because I might call you in a few minutes to have you pick me up."

"Okay, no problem," he says. Another reason why I love my family: They are all so gentle with me. No pressure. So much love and support all the time. My brother gets out of the car and walks around and opens my door. We walk a few feet to the front door of the beautiful Victorian home. I take a deep breath as my brother rings the doorbell. In seconds, the instructor, Donna, comes to the door. I feel like a child on my first day of school.

Donna looks like a writer—definitely an artistic type. She grabs me and hugs me and says, "Welcome, Soyini! We were waiting for you! So glad that you could make it." Donna and my brother talk for a moment and I decide to walk in to meet the rest of the group. I'm relieved because it's a small group of nine ladies. Everyone is nice and very welcoming. My brother comes in and taps me on the shoulder, whispering in my ear that he'll stay in the area for a while and that I should just call if I need him. Thankfully, I don't have to call him until the workshop is over.

Going to the workshop turned out to be one of the best decisions that I've made. It definitely helped snap me out of my depression and gave me a glimmer of hope for the future.

Every day I feel a little bit stronger—not a significant amount stronger—but some days I have a glimmer of hope that keeps me going. The writer's workshop has really inspired me to move toward my future instead of mourning my past. I think a lot about dreams I had before my life changed so drastically. I had been working on building my coaching business. It's a desire I've had for a long time. Because of this, I decide to move forward and look into MBA programs.

After researching schools in my area, I decide to visit a few of them. My good friend Jonathan comes along for emotional support. It's really great having a friend like him. He's a guy I've known since college. From the moment we met in our marketing class, we just clicked. He's definitely an encourager, and I feel very safe with him. My personal safety is always at the forefront of my mind.

I still think back to February 2009, shortly after I was released from the hospital. I definitely couldn't drive, so my parents drove me everywhere I needed to go. My dad would drive, I would be in the passenger seat helping him navigate through the city, and my mom would be in the back seat reminding us of what was on our schedule for the day. We were a perfect team. I had so many doctors' appointments early on, I really don't know what I would have done without my parents. At that time, I was still afraid for my life. I knew that I was alive and safe, and I knew that "he" couldn't attack me again, but I was still terribly afraid for my safety. When you're victimized or attacked like I was, you feel like you have no control. I had never felt that vulnerable in my entire life.

So, riding in the car with my father, I was constantly saying, "Dad, slow down!" Even though my dad drives like 50 mph, I just had this fear of someone hitting us or that we would hit someone. When we would walk down the street, I would watch people closely, and I didn't like strangers to get too close to me. At my home in Maryland, I felt uncomfortable if one of my parents left the front door open for too long or if I saw a strange car in my neighborhood. Looking back, I can see that my survival instincts were still very strong. I also remember thinking that I couldn't believe I was still alive, and that I wanted to control everything in my life to make sure that I was never in danger again. I'm finding that visiting the MBA information sessions is very helpful for me. They help me see that my life will eventually be different. One day, this awful experience will be part of my past. I narrow down my choices to two schools and then eventually down to the one I'll apply to. This one step gives me so much hope for my future. I'm starting to see that I'm slowly building my life one choice at a time. It's been about six months since January 14, and my life is very slowly starting to come together.

I notice that I don't look at my list of questions as much as I used to. Instead, I pray to God a lot and ask to be guided to the next best step for me. And somehow, guidance comes to me in a flash. I might hear a song, or remember an old saying that will serve as a spiritual guidepost.

Sometimes, I really miss my old life in Maryland: my social life, my friends, my home, everything. But it's becoming clear that that was my old life and that life no longer exists. God has placed me on a new path, and as much as I miss my old life, something deep in my spirit lets me know that there has to be something better for me here in California. My mind isn't full of distractions, I'm not stressing about my job, and I have no relationship stress. I can't help but feel that a very fulfilling life is in the making!

In my down moments, I just remind myself to hold on. Years ago, my mother e-mailed me the cutest picture of a little kitten hanging onto a tree branch for dear life. The caption next to the picture read, "Hang in there." I think about that often because there are so many days that I'm just like that cute little kitten, "Hanging on."

For some reason, today I just woke up on the right side of the bed. I feel really good. Not for any specific reason. Nothing has really changed about my situation. I still have a negative balance in the bank (which I honestly laugh about), other bills are stacking up, I face the reality of what I have been through and am still not crystal clear about what the future holds for me, but despite all of that, I feel really good inside—like I'm bubbling over with joy. This is my own sign that lets me know when God is with me. Actually, I've learned that He's always with me, but I've really availed myself of His presence today.

I've been taking my relaxing walk around the marina. I'm just having a moment where I take it all in, especially the sound of the waves hitting the shore . It's such a peaceful sound as the fresh air hits my noise. The beauty of nature just doing what it does is always such a healing experience. I see this same view a few times a week, but for some reason today, I really appreciate it even more. It's as if the ocean seems to wipe away all of my worries, as if nature just wraps me up in a blanket of universal love. All of life's problems seem so trivial in comparison with the big picture of why we are here.

Life is really a gift. It feels good to have time and peace of mind to really experience why we are here. Moments like this are priceless. I can't put into words everything that I'm feeling, but I definitely feel so good. So connected. So peaceful. I just sit on the bench and sip my bottle of water and continue to let my worries wash away into the infinite ocean. This is my sacred time with God. I'm starting to see life in a way that I haven't seen it before. It's amazing how much of life we miss when we are so busy living and taking care of business. So much is here that we can't see until we have time to slow down and just be where we are.

I'm having lots of good days—I've had about six good days in a row. My talks with my therapist are helping, as well as getting out with friends and doing normal things—activities that I used to do. I can't help but study everyone around me. I lost a level of naivety when he shot me. I won't ever look at people the same. I know that some folks can be dangerous. I'm still very skeptical of new people who come into my life. Truthfully, I'm just not ready for new people, and I'm fine with that decision. It's only been about seven and a half months, so I think I should feel this way.

This time of being with my SELF and not having any distractions is very important. I'm starting to see that everything is literally being cleared out so that I can see what's really here. It's as if God is removing all the things from my life that I thought were permanent and important, and now he has just left me with me—no job, no money in the bank, no definite plans, no pressure, no stress. Just me, like I have a clean slate right now. I'm able to kind of step back and see me. I'm especially thankful for being back with my family, because so much of myself was lost over the years is being restored here at home.

Prior to the shooting, my life was too full with people and stuff. I couldn't see what's really here. I gave away so much of my energy and so much of myself that I lost parts of me. Now, I'm thankful for every day that I have. Every day, I'm letting go of parts of the old me that I no longer need. My spirit is shifting on the inside. I really didn't need as much as I thought I needed—including having men in my life.

Romantic relationships have always been a big distraction for me. If I wasn't in a relationship, I was working on getting one. As I got older, I desired the stability of a relationship, but some of the guys that I was with weren't necessarily the best for me. They weren't bad men, they just weren't for me.

Now, I feel a deep sense of acceptance for the way my life is. For the first time in my life, I don't want to fix anything. I'm happy with my life. I'm so close to God that I feel His presence in my life all of the time. I've never felt this way before—it's like a rebirth. It's much deeper than just having a happy day—my entire being feels like it's shifting to a new level. I even see life differently. I'm building up a confidence in myself and in my life that I've never known. Nothing around me is necessarily changing, but on the inside I'm changing rapidly. It's a difficult experience to describe, but it's happening and I feel it. I feel like a visitor in my own body.

There is a stillness that I feel in my spirit. I feel very calm and very sure of everything that is coming to me in the form of guidance from God. I'm not pushing or forcing things to happen, I'm simply allowing. I'm trusting my spirit to let me know when it's time to make certain moves, and when it's time to be still.

I'm still waking up and having good days. I wake up after a good night's rest, and I feel like something negative left my body and was replaced with unconditional love. I'm not sure what prayer I prayed or what thoughts or beliefs I acquired, but whatever is happening, it's working. I decide to just go with it and not question the process. Plus, it feels so good to have good days. God knows that I've had my share of bad days. I've even noticed that my dreams are starting to change. I'm not having as many nightmares anymore, and when "he" is in my dreams, I'm not afraid anymore.

August 2009

It's August now, and I fully realize that I'm living a brand new life. I wake up daily with the realization that everything I've built over the years is gone. All I can do is move forward. I look in the mirror, and I see a different person too. There is still a bit of swelling in my face and a few very small scars here and there, but I remind myself that this is the new me. My scars are a constant reminder of the amazing things God can do in your life. Even when I start to feel sorry for myself, which I do from time to time, I realize that I'm still here for a reason. I've gotten to the point where I purposefully avoid mirrors and I shun pictures. The few times that I get out with my friends, it seems like everyone has a camera. I used to enjoy cameras, but I don't anymore.

On this particular Monday morning in August 2009, I wake up rather early—about 7 a.m. The house is quiet, and I appreciate the stillness. For some reason, I go and stand in front of the mirror. I look at the woman staring back at me, and I realize that this is the first time I've actually "SEEN" myself in about seven or eight months. Up until this point, I'd catch a quick glance of myself in the mirror, but I'd never just stare. So today, I see me.

I look deep into my eyes. I study my hair line that was shaved for surgery, and I kind of laugh at the little sprouts of hair that are trying to make their way back. Because my hair hasn't grown back all the way, the stitches across my head are still visible, and they run basically from ear to ear. I think the doctors had to pull back my scalp when they were operating. But my hair has grown enough that when I wear it down, it covers the stitches. I study the small, almost invisible scar in between my eyebrows that is the result of my falling onto the cement after being shot. I study my nose and my mouth. I remember how crooked my mouth was for about two months after the incident—I looked like I'd had a stroke. My mouth was so crooked that I sounded different when I spoke—my words were all slurred. One of the doctors told me that I might need to get more surgery to straighten out my mouth, but today, my mouth looks the way it used to look. It's completely back to normal. Next, my gaze moves over to my left jaw. The swelling has gone down a lot, and I have another small scar from the surgery I underwent to have the fragments of the bullet removed. I then look at my right eye. I have a prosthetic eye now because my real eye had to be removed. The prosthetic actually looks really good. I still have to get used to it, but that's getting easier every day. Next, I step back a few inches from the mirror and take in everything.

What a miracle! I had honestly been avoiding mirrors because I didn't feel like I was pretty anymore. I had become self-conscious over the past few months. Don't get me wrong—I've never been obsessed with my looks, not even remotely obsessed with my looks. But I have always considered myself an attractive woman. After something so ugly and evil happened to me, I knew that I looked different. In my mind I felt that anyone who saw me knew exactly what happened to me, and I guess that made me feel less attractive, so I avoided mirrors for months. Mirrors were also a reality check—a painful reminder of what happened.

But I tell myself that today is a new day. I see that I really do look like my old self. And then it hits me—this is the face of a woman who God loved so much that He decided to keep me here. I feel beyond blessed to have this realization. I give myself the best and biggest smile that I can give, and I just stare at the mirror a little longer. Each moment I stare at my reflection helps me take in this new awareness so much deeper. I feel beyond beautiful, and I decide that I'll never feel self-conscious about my looks or what happened to me again. My scars are my new beauty marks. I fully embrace this new awareness of me. I feel a deep sense of confidence, so I say out loud, "This is the new me, and I love the new me."

September 2009

I have been so much like my "old" self lately. I've been catching up with friends and thinking about the future a lot. And I've been content doing nothing except getting a lot of rest. When I feel like working on something or being a little productive, I start working on my grad school application. But I'm also looking forward to going back to Maryland for a few days. I have some follow-up doctors' visits to attend to and I'm going to see my East Coast friends. We're going to celebrate my birthday, and believe me—this is a birthday that I'm extra excited to have!

It's the end of September and I'm ready for my trip, even if this trip to Maryland has been a stretch for me. Up until this point, I've always had someone around me, whether it's a family member or a friend. I'm truly never really alone. But I will be for this trip, and I feel ready to make the more-than 3,000-mile flight on my own. When my father drops me off at the airport, I feel like a kindergartener on my first day of school. This is such a big step for me. I tell myself that I'm ready to conquer my fear of being by myself, and I remind myself that I am safe.

I sleep for most of the long flight, but I also talk to my chatty neighbor sitting next to me. His name is Scott and he's a traveling salesman from Dallas. He looks like he's between 45 and 50 years old. His hair is a dark sandy brown sprinkled with gray. He wears glasses and he has the most piercing blue eyes I've ever seen. Scott's on his way to Baltimore for some type of conference. He inquires about my trip to Baltimore, but I just tell him that I'm going to visit friends—there's no way I'm going to go into my life story. But, Scott's a talker, and he feels comfortable telling me his life story.

He confides in me that he's starting over in life. He was married for 22 years and has three daughters. Apparently he's lost it all because I can see the sadness in his eyes. He tells me that he had been an alcoholic for many years, and the disease caused the destruction of his family and his life. It got so bad that he lost his job, family, friends, and his self-respect. It seems like he goes on for hours telling me about his troubles, but I don't interrupt him because I know that he needs to be heard .

"It's never too late to start over," he says in a very confident voice. Then he tells me that he's ready to deal with his pain in a healthier way instead of using alcohol to drown his pain. I'll probably never see Scott again, but I feel like I got to know him so much during that flight. He lost everything and now, in his late 40s or 50s, he's starting over. Although we had two totally different life experiences that caused us to start over, I really understand him when he says, "It's never too late to start over." I saw that as a sign for me to realize that all of us are going to be met with challenges in life, but it's up to us to pick ourselves up and keep going. I know that one day, Scott will have his family in his life again, and he'll rebuild a great life. And I know that I'll get everything back that I lost. I just have to remember to never give up.

After we land in Baltimore, I walk to baggage claim and I just look around at all the people. I can't believe that I'm here by myself. For a quick moment I panic because I see someone who looks like "him." When I have these moments, I have to literally stop whatever I'm doing and realize that I am safe. I have to talk myself through it for a minute, realize where I am, and quietly repeat I am safe. As I walk through the terminal, so many memories flash through my mind. I think about times that he picked me up from that exact airport. I would have never in my wildest dreams thought that things would turn out the way they did.

When my friend Andrea arrives to pick me up from the airport, we laugh and talk the whole ride back to her house. We're both from the Bay Area, and we moved to the East Coast around the same time. When I lived in Maryland and was missing California, I'd hang out with Andrea and I'd feel like I had a piece of home with me.

Andrea is very short, maybe five feet tall. (Okay, I'll give her five foot one so she doesn't get mad at me.) She's very lively and expressive when she talks—just a fun person to be around. When my parents flew in to Baltimore on January 15th, Andrea was there to pick them up. Somehow she had gotten in touch with my parents and arranged everything, and they also stayed with her that first night. She made sure that everything went smoothly for my parents while they were at the hospital with me. I can never thank her enough for being there for my parents during such a difficult time. She's a great friend.

The first night I'm here, we just hang out and catch up on everything that's been going on. Then we put the final touches on my "mini" birthday party happening Thursday night in DC. I'm not usually into birthdays, but this is a special one, so I'm extra excited.

When I was younger, my mother did a great job planning my birthday parties. I had one every year up until I was 13. There were plenty of slumber parties, skating parties, and Chuck E. Cheese's when I was really small. I used to think that everyone's mom planned parties for them, but as I got older, I saw that wasn't the norm for everyone. Because I'm the oldest child, my mother and father put a lot of energy and love into me, and I've always felt loved and wanted. My mom has a "baby book" for me that she created to track all of my early birthdays and my "first" moments. I've always felt that the most important thing parents can do for a child is provide a loving and nurturing home environment for them. Childhood is your introduction to life and really impacts the way you live your life. As I've gotten older, I can see how those early years affected my character and self-esteem. We weren't rich, but that didn't matter to me. I always had what I needed, and I always had a lot of love.

My birthday is here! My good friend Tonia has driven down from Delaware. Tonia is one of the most stylish women I know. She always looks effortlessly put together. I don't know how she does it, but she does it every time. She's tall and very slim. Tonia is such a caring and loyal friend, the type of friend who feels your pain. She's such a sweetheart.

My parents have given me a little birthday money to spend, and I invite Tonia to help me put it to good use. I go to my old hair salon and get my hair done. Then Tonia and I go to the makeup counter to get our faces done. I really want to look good for my birthday. I've never been into wearing too much makeup—a little lip gloss, eye shadow every once in a while, and I can probably count the number of times that I've worn blush.

So Tonia and I hit the makeup counter. Tonia tells the lady, "It's my girl's birthday today and we want her to look FAB-ULOUS!" So I sit down in the chair, and Tonia and I begin picking out colors for my eyes, lips, and cheeks. When my makeup is finished, the lady hands me a mirror. I love the makeup, and I can see that it's really going to look great with my outfit that I've already picked out. I'm so excited that I almost cry, but I remember that I don't want to mess up the beautiful smoky eye that she's created for me or the blush on my cheeks.

This day is working out just the way I planned: I wanted to look great for my birthday, and I didn't want to worry about anything from the past. I just wanted to enjoy life and have fun with my friends. I had struggled with my looks in previous months until I had my moment of acceptance, but now, I feel like I'm back. I haven't dressed up in months, nor have I worried too much about my appearance. It feels good to be a girly girl again.

My party turns out great! I hang out with friends the way that I used to, and I don't worry or think about anything from the past. I'm just in the moment, having fun and creating memories!

My remaining days in Maryland are full of catching up with friends and taking care of some outstanding business. As I go back to the Baltimore airport, I feel so energized. I'm satisfied knowing that I successfully traveled on my own. I almost hate to leave, but at this point I kind of miss my family. It's time to head back west.

October 2009

Today marks the nine-month anniversary of the shooting, and it's turning out to be a good month. For some reason, I feel like this is a lucky month. Nine months has marked the birth of new life for me. I feel like all of my prayers for peace are starting to come together. I don't have as many bad days as I was having. I don't worry as much as I did. I have more energy now to begin to take steps toward my future. I don't allow myself to spend too much time thinking about money and bills; instead, I write and daydream about the future. The light at the end of the tunnel is starting to get a little bit brighter. I'm learning how faith works because there's no actual evidence that things are changing—I just have to trust that they will. On the outside, my bank account is still negative, and I have bill collectors calling and mailing me letters daily. But, despite that, I believe this is all temporary. Somehow, I just know that a brighter day is coming. SOON.

I feel like God is telling me, "Hold on. Don't give up. I'm with you." I'm learning how to give a situation or problem over to God, to release things and not hold on as much as I used to. I don't have the same level of fear that I had prior to January 14. I trust God so much more when I pray. I see that God works in the most subtle ways. My prayers are even different. I'm more clear when I talk to God. Instead of asking for "things," I ask for qualities, like peace, love, grace, and faith. I ask for the strength to get from one phase of this experience to the next one. And it's working.

November 2009

I have passed my 10-month mark. Every time I realize that another month has passed, I just can't believe it. The whole experience is surreal. Even though I do think I'm coping better, I still have a few bad days when I just feel sad about how much my life has changed, and I have moments where I'm so tired of being broke. I'm so strapped, and I feel like my options are so limited. You can't really have too much fun if you don't have money.

I'm also still discovering other ways that my life has been altered. When I went to the DMV to renew my license, I found out that because my vision has changed, I have to take the written test again and I have to take the behind-the-wheel driving test. I am beyond frustrated. For one, I don't have the funds to pay for all of this, and secondly, it's not my fault that my vision changed—it's HIS.

When I left the DMV today, I just cried. I sat in the car for about an hour and cried. I couldn't even move. When the tears come now, they're so powerful.

"It's just not fair!" I keep saying this aloud and to myself as I think about all the changes I've made over the past 10 months. How much more can I take? I'm tired of making adjustments. As I sit in the car, I'm extra gentle with myself. I let myself cry, and then I just sit in the stillness for a while. I don't hold back sadness anymore. I release everything.

I finished my application for grad school and my interview is scheduled. I tell myself that even if I don't get in, I'm already a winner. The fact that I endured a major tragedy in the same year that I'm applying to grad school, that I'm ready to get myself back together again, is amazing to me. I can't help but wonder where this strength is coming from. Sometimes I can't believe myself, and I'm certain that it's not just me.

In the letter from the university, I'm instructed to plan on being in the interview for one hour. My gosh, that sounds like an eternity to me. What will we talk about all of that time? I hope I can get through this. Then I remind myself if I can survive the night of January 14, 2009, then I can survive anything. That's the one benefit to experiencing such a tragedy: You fully understand there is nothing that can break you. Tragedy brings an awareness of what you're really made of. It takes away the fear. Tragedy puts everything in life in perspective. Tragedy helps you see how temporary everything truly is.

I decide to wear my favorite grey suit. It's two years old but very stylish. However, two years ago, I was a lot more active and in shape, so the suit fit me perfectly. Fast forward two years, and the suit fits more snugly. I can't even button the pants, and it's clinging more to my legs than it ever clung before.

My weight has fluctuated this year. Before the shooting, I was in good shape—lean with good muscle definition. After I was released from the hospital, I lost lots of curves and weight because I wasn't eating. Then by the summer, I was eating again and I wasn't as active as I used to be, so I got back to my normal size plus I gained some "extra"—all in the wrong places it seems. But, hey, I give myself a pass. It's been a tough year. Luckily, I'm tall—five foot ten—so I can handle a few extra pounds without looking like I gained weight. Thank God for height. So I decide to put on my girdle (that I bought to help me handle these extra pounds around the middle) and wear my favorite blouse with my suit and get going.

On the way to the interview, I listen to my favorite music (read Michael Jackson) and I say a prayer before entering the campus. I arrive 20 minutes early and just sit in the car and take it all in. It's a Catholic college, so I feel such a sense of peace being here. I'm not Catholic, but the campus is beautiful and peaceful—it works for me. It's a great program, and I just feel good when I'm here.

When I get out of the car, though, the button on my pants pops off . I look around to see if anyone notices, then I try to fix it really quickly. Luckily, I have a pin that I use to temporarily pin my pants in place. Thank God I have my briefcase/portfolio to put in front of me to distract from my exploding pants. As I enter the administration building, I'm a little nervous, so I go to the restroom and splash water on my face. I tell myself again that no matter what, I'm proud of myself for coming this far. I also say a quick prayer to God to ask that I don't have any wardrobe malfunctions while I'm in my interview.

So I sit on the Victorian style couches in the waiting area for about five minutes before the admissions director comes out to greet me. As I stand up to shake his hand, I pray that my button doesn't pop again. I also make sure that my jacket will cover anything else that could go wrong.

I'm interviewed by two people, and I'm extremely nervous in the beginning of the interview, but after a few moments I calm down and let them see the real me. They both know what I've been through because I wrote about it a little bit in my statement of purpose. My interview lasts about 30 minutes. When I leave, I sit in the car and take a deep breath—then I panic a little bit.

"Oh my God," I think, "that interview was supposed to be one hour. Maybe they didn't like me. Maybe they thought I wasn't a good fit for the program. Maybe they didn't think I was ready." The doubt comes pouring in, so I call my parents and a few friends to debrief with them. Everyone agrees that the interviewers probably heard everything they needed to hear in order to make a decision, and they tell me not to worry.

"I sure hope I get in," I say to myself. At the end of the interview, I asked, "When will you let me know your decision?" and I got the whole, "Don't call us, we'll call you" answer.

I am accepted to grad school!! I'm beyond excited. I can't believe it. I went in for my interview on Wednesday, and it's Saturday, and I have my acceptance letter. This is a much-needed victory for me and a step in the right direction for my future. This solidifies my desire to take control of my future and redefine myself. My family and I are jumping up and down with excitement. My friends are excited! We're all feeling good.

Everyone around me has been on this journey with me. They've seen me endure the darkest days of my life, and they've watched me be so close to giving up. Now, they can see that the light at the end of the tunnel is getting brighter and brighter. I think that my loved ones needed to see me have some great things happen in my life too.

It's amazing how much this acceptance letter has increased my faith even more. I feel like this is a sign from God letting me know that He's still watching over me. He wants me to know that my future is going to be very bright. This is perfect because in January 2010 I won't be Soyini Taylor, the young lady who was shot in front of her home. I will be Soyini Taylor, the survivor and the grad student. I'll be living a new life. It's a great moment, so I just take it all in.

I'm still taking it easy; it's fall and life is slowing down. One thing I loved about living on the East Coast was the experience of the seasons. Fall is my favorite time of year because—for one thing—I was born in the fall. Plus, I love the way the trees looked in Maryland, that beautiful mix of gold, red, and orange. The temperatures start to cool off in the fall, but it's not cold yet. It's the perfect weather of the year, like nature is just giving us all a chance to relax after an active summer.

Summer was so alive in Maryland! Everyone was out all day and night. And the days were so long—it would be light outside until about 8:30 p.m. The air was humid and sticky, which would always give my skin that natural glow, but which also meant two or three showers per day! I love wearing flip-flops in the summertime too. My feet feel free when they're exposed, and my favorite thing to do in the summer is go to the beach and walk barefoot in the sand.

Winter in Maryland, though, wasn't one of my favorite times. Growing up in California, I never had to deal with snow, so that was like an adventure. Living in California, we would "go to the snow" in Lake Tahoe or someplace like that, but on the East Coast, snow is an inevitable part of life. I still laugh to myself because every winter I'd tell my friends I was moving back to California because I couldn't take another East Coast winter. Yeah, I said that every year for like nine years.

But there is some beauty to the winter, and it definitely slows you down. The snow looks beautiful on the trees, and it feels peaceful being in the warm indoors watching the snow fall outside. As winter winds down, I'm reminded why spring is another one of my favorite seasons.

As we enter spring, my body and spirit are prepared to jump out in a big way in life. I feel an extra sense of ambition as I watch nature unfold right in front of my eyes, and the trees come alive and flowers slowly start to blossom. I feel that my spirit is going through a similar transformation. The temperature starts rising, and nature just seems to get moving. In Washington, DC, I always liked watching the cherry blossoms come out in the spring. They are absolutely breathtaking. People would come from all over the country and the world to watch the cherry blossoms bloom.

This fall in California, a good friend of mind has invited me to a Buddhist half-day retreat. Although I'm not Buddhist, I agree to go to get a different perspective. I have to admit that since the shooting and its aftermath, I'm constantly searching for answers everywhere. One thing I've noticed in life is that all of the answers we need are already here—it's just important to be open and available to receive them. I have understood life better by reading about many different religions and spiritual practices. I haven't closed myself off to any religion because I've found truth in many of them.

So today, I'm at this Buddhist half-day retreat with one of my friends. It's at this beautiful center in Redwood City, California. Everyone is dressed "normal," and they look like people I see in the mall or at restaurants. There is a regular group of about 20 people here today and a teacher, plus a few of us who are new. The instructor looks to be in his late 50s with grey hair that's balding at the top. He's dressed in jeans and a white shirt. Apparently, he's not the teacher who normally holds the retreat and is just filling in today.

My friend and I are greeted by a lady who whispers and asks if we are familiar with meditation. We both answer yes, so she says okay. Then she goes on to inform us of the agenda for the morning, and I can see it includes lots of meditation time. When I walk into the room where the teacher and students are, I take a seat on the floor. The soft-spoken lady seems to read my mind and walks over to hand me a cushion for my bottom. Thank God, I think to myself. It's so quiet in this room that I swear you can hear a pin drop.

The teacher soon breaks the silence and greets the group. He opens a book and reads us a few paragraphs about the importance of meditation and stillness. He informs us that we are going to start with 45-minute meditation. I cut my friend a look like, "What? A 45-minute meditation?"

Oh man, I think to myself, this is going to be a long day. I have definitely been a fan of meditation and have practiced it for years, but for some reason today, that 45 minutes sounds like a long time. What if I have to get up and go to the bathroom? What if I'm overcome with emotion and have to cry like a baby? I'm not going to feel comfortable doing that here. I wonder if it's too late to leave. I have a million thoughts flashing through my mind when I realize the teacher has finished talking and everyone around me has their eyes closed and are deep in their "meditative state." I look at my friend to the right of me, and she's also in her zone. Oh well, I think, let me get ready for my 45 minutes of silence.

I get lost in my thoughts and my mind races. I notice that I keep creating moments of anxiety. What if my car gets towed? I think I'm hungry. After a while, I decide to stop thinking and really try to clear my mind. I never realized before how hard it is to do—and think—nothing. After what seems like only a second, I hear the chimes go off, alerting everyone that it's time to end the meditation. As I slowly open my eyes and look around the room, everyone looks so refreshed and calm all at the same time.

Our next exercise is to practice a mindfulness walk. Oh great, I think to myself, I definitely know how to walk. I've always loved a brisk walk or a jog when I have to get my mind off of things. So, I think, I can definitely do this. Then the lady with the soft voice asks my friend, me, and a few other new folks if we know how to walk. I think we all kind of look at her like, "Duh, of course we do." Unfazed by our unspoken expression, she explains that the mindfulness practice is designed to bring you into the moment and get you really present with yourself. Or something like that. Oh my God, I think to myself, not another meditation. So she shows us how to walk at a very slow pace: we slowly lift one leg and take a very small, almost-still step forward then alternate with the other leg. We're taking very slow, deliberate steps, and we do this in one straight line with each person being totally into their own space. I'm surprised no one bumps into the person in front of them. We kind of walk in one huge circle inside the Buddhist Center then we're informed that we can also go outside if we need more space. My friend stays inside, but I decide to go out, and get some fresh air.

When I get outside, there are three other people out here doing the mindfulness walk. I join them for a few moments, but I honestly get bored. I like stillness and quiet, but this is just too much. So I decide to do what is natural for me—I do my own thing and walk around the neighborhood a few times. The Buddhist Center is in this lovely, quiet neighborhood with tall, beautiful trees lining each side of the street. It's so quiet that I can hear birds chirping. This is a perfect neighborhood for a nice walk, I think to myself.

As I begin walking, I realize this is what my spirit needed. I'm comfortable, so I walk and walk and walk some more. I check out the neighborhood as if I'm going on a walking tour or something. Then my intuition tells me to go back to the center and catch up to the others, and when I get back to the center, it's just like clockwork. It's as if I knew exactly when everyone was going to be finishing up. My intuition has saved me so many times in life. I'll never forget how clearly my intuition spoke to me the night of January 14. It literally guided me step by step on how to help save my life.

I've always been intuitive, but I haven't always trusted what I heard. At this point in my life, I'm committed to trusting my "inner voice." When I really think about it, my intuition or inner guidance has never let me down. Never. The only time when I feel let down is when I don't listen.

We finish up at the half-day retreat with another meditation and a short talk about suffering. This whole concept of suffering keeps coming up. I'm starting to feel like it's something I might want to investigate. After the talk, we have opportunities to ask questions, and then we're each asked if we can help straighten up the center. I vacuum, and my friend sweeps. We all pitch in to keep this center looking beautiful. All in all, my half-day retreat at this center was pretty fun. I actually do feel a lot more relaxed. I feel very light.

I've been having so many great days—and then I start worrying about money, and I start feeling really down about everything that's happened to me. Out of nowhere, these thoughts hit me like a ton of bricks, and the emotional pain is so heavy. Every time I think about the fact that my life was almost taken, sadness overwhelms me. I can't control these emotions at all. I just cry and let out the sadness. That familiar question keeps passing through my mind, "Why me?" and I immediately think back to a conversation I had with a friend of mine two or three weeks ago.

I remember saying to him, "Why did this have to happen to me?"

"Why not you?" he asked, without even thinking about it. If he wasn't my good friend, I probably would have slapped him for making that statement. But, he went on to say that we all have challenges and storms in our lives. It's God's way of preparing us for something bigger and better in our future. He told me that maybe God's plan for my life was so big that I needed to have some things in my character sharpened. Maybe I needed to get rid of some old ways. Maybe I needed a fresh start. Then he reminded me that God definitely wants me to be here for a reason, and that He knows how much I can handle. My friend also told me that once I've gotten through this season in my life, I'll be exactly where God wants me to be. Some of what my friend says definitely sounds true, but the whole situation still sucks to me .

Today is Friday, the day my brothers and I hang out. I always look forward to Fridays. We're going to eat at one of my favorite restaurants, and then we're going to the movies. Although I never planned to be living at home at this point in my life, I'm thankful for the time I have to reconnect with my family. When I'm with them, I feel such a sense of joy. Sometimes, I wonder how this has affected my brothers. When I have to cry and complain, they're always here to listen to me. My father has also been such a rock. My whole family keeps me encouraged. They always inspire me and tell me that everything is going to be fine.

The thought that always keeps me pushing is that everything in life is temporary. No phase of life lasts forever. The good times are temporary and the bad times are temporary. During the times when I can barely hold on, I focus on this idea. Somewhere deep in my spirit, I'm starting to understand that I'm really living a new life. All the life skills or tools that I used in the past are obsolete. I no longer want to live that old life. Maybe it is possible that God has something bigger planned for me. If that's the case, then I don't want to screw this up. I'm committed to realizing this vision that God has for me.

I begin to surrender all of my desires to God. I've heard this term surrender for years, but I didn't understand how to really do it. I'm learning that it isn't really something that you do. For me, it's just a way of letting go. So I'm just letting go of a lot of energy that no longer serves me. I'm letting go of my desire to have things figured out. I'm letting go of things that

I used to think were so important to me. I've learned that the more I push to keep things together financially and otherwise, the harder it is for me to keep going. So I do what I can and I let go of the worry. I can't allow worry about money to kill me.

Now that I've spent about 10 months really being with myself with no distractions at all, I recognize subtle ways that I used to sabotage myself. I made my relationships with men more important than anything else in my life. I always wanted to know what my purpose in life was. I always said that I wanted to do my life's work, but my actions didn't always measure up. Whenever I was about to get on my life's path, the distractions would come—I'd meet some new guy and I would place all of my energy in him. Then I'd be angry when I didn't get the "love" from him that I expected. I was committed to so many things, but I wasn't committed to myself. Looking back, I can see how my lack of commitment to myself allowed me to make choices that weren't always the healthiest.

I'm learning that a strong commitment to yourself and to God have to be the first commitments you make in life. It's all part of your foundation. Somehow, I realize that God is strengthening my character and taking my weaknesses and sharpening them. My character is being fine-tuned every day. Now that the desire to be in a relationship isn't the most important thing for me, I am left with me. I see why people, both men and women, run from being alone or lonely, but there is a big difference between being alone and being lonely. When you're by yourself and you feel lonely, that's a problem because we should all be able to enjoy our time alone. It's a very necessary part of being alive. Everyone at some point in their life has to be comfortable in their own skin.

When you feel like you aren't good enough by yourself, you constantly seek out validation from other people to make you feel like you are enough. And no one can or should have to do that but you. Even with all of the personal development and spiritual work that I've done over the years, I realize that I was really lacking self-love and self-commitment. But that's all going to change.

Each and every day now, I'm consciously focused on the fact that I'm perfect and whole just as I am. I can tell that I'm filling up a void that has lived in my heart forever. The missing thing in my life was "me." I see this all so clearly now that it makes me cry. I think about all the years I wasted running from one relationship to the next, searching for this "thing," this feeling, but all along the way, I just needed to stop and love myself. God, I wish that it wouldn't have taken all of this for me to begin to see my life so clearly.

I still don't know what my future will look like because nothing around me is really changing, but I'm certainly growing and developing rapidly. I'm seeing so much of who I really am. I'm shedding the old me, and making way for the new me. At times I feel like a different person because I'm unfamiliar with all of the new choices that I'm making. But, I know that I'm doing a lot of things right. My future will be better because I am better.

December 2009

This month has been so rocky. Holidays are usually tough for me if I'm not in a relationship. This year is a little different though because I realize that I am different—I no longer place all of my energy into relationships. The times when I do think about it, I just focus on a healthier thought.

I have thought about the fact that we all have "gifts" that are God given. When God blesses us with our gifts, we're not meant to hold on to them. We're meant to share them. We don't own our "gifts"—God does, so when you think about it, they aren't even ours to hold on to. Some people's gifts are more evident than others'. Some people are good singers or performers. Some people have other "gifts" like the gift of encouragement or inspiration. We should use these gifts because they all help make the world a better place.

Even with the holidays, this month has been going by pretty slowly. I've been feeling down a lot too. Memories are coming back: I think about how in December 2008 I was glad to be home with my family here in California because I was terrified to be in Maryland. He was still stalking me and calling me like a crazy person. I remember how I never had peace when I was at my home in Maryland. In the back of my mind, I knew that any day could be the day "he" would decide to act out his anger and craziness. I think about how the restraining order that I filed didn't seem to protect or prevent anything from happening. In some cases it might actually help, but for me, it did nothing. There was nothing that would keep him from doing what he had planned to do.

So today, on December 24, 2009, I let out my biggest cry. From the bottom of my soul, I just cry and mourn for myself. I cry for the part of me that's endured so much in 2008. I cry tears of joy that I made it through that nightmare. And I cry because I can't wait for 2009 to be over. During this entire time, while I'm having what I've come to call "my end of 2009 emotional release," my parents are right next to me. My mom's on the left of me, stroking my hand, and my dad's on my right, passing me tissues and helping me wipe away my tears. There's no conversation between us, but I know in my heart that they understand everything I want to say. They're simply here for me, loving me and allowing me to have my experience.

As my tears subside, my father says, "Well, at least you know that 2010 can only get better." Then he makes some joke about all of the tissue that I've gone through this year. His joke allows the three of us to get the biggest laugh and relax a little.

With this emotional release behind me, I'm counting down the days to 2010. When I sit down and think about all of the possibilities for my future, I'm just happy. I've learned some really powerful lessons, and I've let go of so many beliefs and thoughts that have held me back in the past. I feel more confident and strong in my body. I finally feel safe, and I know that I don't have to worry about being attacked like that again. The memories and dreams might haunt me every so often, but I know that I'm very safe now.

One technique that I always use when it's time to forgive is I take out a bunch of paper and make sure I'm in a space where I won't be interrupted. I turn off the phone, clear out all distractions, and then I just write. I forgive myself for judging myself as _____, and I fill in the blank. I also forgive other people when I need to do that too. But in the beginning, I focus on me because forgiveness starts with me.

The key for me is to write as fast as I can so that I don't try to edit anything. I want to be as "in the moment" as possible. I never go back and look at what I've written because once it's on paper, the release is already done. Plus, I don't want to be tempted to erase something or edit it so that it sounds nicer. I want everything to be raw. In the end, I'm amazed by how much comes out.

When I finish writing, I tear up all of the paper. Some people actually burn the paper, but you have to make sure that you can do that safely. You don't want that to be the reason your house burns down.

December/January 2009

It's New Year's Eve 2009. I've never been so excited to put one year behind me as I am right now. My family and I have plans to go visit some relatives who live about two hours north of the Bay Area. My friends are calling and texting me to coordinate plans for this evening, but I'm not really interested in celebrating the way I used to. I feel like I have permission to move beyond this nightmare of 2009. I'm just looking forward to writing the words "January 1, 2010" on paper.

This year of 2009 has been incredible. I'm exhausted from all of the changes this year has brought me—so many challenges, so many tests, so much of everything. I'm tired. But the thought of a new year gives me the ability to perk up and be positive about the future.

We are at my aunt Margaret's house, and she's prepared an amazing dinner for us. My aunt and uncle have a beautiful, spacious home. The ceilings are high and the space is very open. The dining room and kitchen overlook a golf course that's part of their very private community. A marble table sits in the center of the kitchen and functions as a serving area.

My aunt has prepared three different types of chicken: baked, teriyaki, and fried. She's also cooked some catfish. Because that side of the family is from Mississippi, we have some special catfish from Mississippi—it's so fresh and so light I pile as much of it on my plate as possible. There's also a good-looking beef dish, but I'm not a fan of red meat so I pass it up. Then there's the pan of baked beans with just the right amount of brown sugar to add a little kick to it and a huge dish of freshly cooked string beans. There's potato salad, a green salad, steamed carrots and a warm batch of rolls. Oh, and then there is dessert. I love dessert! There's the freshly baked pound cake and homemade ice cream. And then there's my personal favorite, homemade sweet potato pie. Yummy. Since I was a little kid, I've loved sweet potato pie. My aunt Margaret always makes me my own pie for the holiday, and I always say I'm going to share it, but that never really happens. I eat as much as I want today because we're celebrating.

After dinner, I help my aunt with the dishes and we catch up on what's been happening since the last time we talked. I love talking to my aunt Margaret because she's one of the unofficial family historians. She tells me so much about my grandparents and my great-great-grandparents. The more I discover about my family, the more I understand myself. When the dishes are done, the men watch football and the women chat about current events and listen to music. Somewhere in there, I take a quick nap.

When we get home that evening, I decide to write down a few things that were positive for 2009. As usual, I'm grateful to be alive, but so much of this year has sucked. Anyway, I find some things that I can honestly say that I'm grateful for. I also tell myself that 2010 and beyond are going to be very simple for me. I'm going to focus on rebuilding my life one step at a time—no big, huge goals, just little, small steps. Along the way, I'll check in with myself and determine what I need to do next.

In my spirit, I feel peaceful. I'm already starting to feel lighter as 2009 becomes my past. I've decided to stay home tonight and just take in the experience of being here to see another year. And here's the countdown: 5, 4, 3, 2, 1—HAPPY NEW YEAR! I take a deep breath and say to myself, I made it. It never ceases to amaze me that there is still part of me that can't believe I really survived such a tragic event. When I think about falling down onto the cold cement on January 14, 2009, to fighting for my life in the hospital, to having to learn how to swallow again, to losing my eye, I can't believe that I'm still here. It's a humbling experience that brings tears to my eyes—tears of joy because I can now officially say that I've lived to see 2010.

Now I'm counting down to my next big milestone—the one-year anniversary. My official rebirth, January 14, 2010. When the day arrives, it's surreal. Exactly one year ago today my life changed forever. I wake up early, 7 a.m. California time, and I think back to one year prior in Maryland. I had no idea that my life was just hours away from changing forever. That night, I arrived home at approximately 9:55 p.m. Eastern Standard Time. So at 6:55 p.m. Pacific Time I take a moment of silence for my spirit. I thank God for my life and I tell myself that I can relax now and move forward. Three days later, I'm in grad school.

Life is truly amazing .

Present Day

Things are a lot different now. After much contemplation, I decided to move back to Maryland. I am on another faith walk. I have my MBA in one hand, but no job or place to live back in Maryland. I have managed to keep my house through all of the change, but I am renting it out to tenants. I am determined to move back to Maryland and am eager to start my life over. I have a strong feeling that my destiny is in Maryland. My target date to move back is July 15, 2011.

At the last minute, literally 3 weeks before I am all set to move, a former coworker said that I can come and stay with him and his family while I get back on my feet. This turned out to be nothing short of a miracle. On the inside, I am nervous, because I have no idea of how this will work out. I need to find a job, decide on where I am going to live and maybe find love. I just pray that things will work out.

When I arrive to the BWI airport on 7/15/11, I can't believe that I am back. I feel a tear run down my left check. The reality that I have moved back to a place that left me with so many memories. The place that raised me. The place where I almost lost my life. The place that still feels like home.

Well, I am here. My friend picks me up from the airport. Bernard is a former coworker from Xerox who I worked with several years ago. He has always been a kind and genuine person. Bernard always has a smile on his face and something positive to say. In the car, he greats me and says welcome back to the East Coast, Soy!

The trip back to my new home feels so surreal. Part of me doubts myself and I wonder if I can really make it out here. Bernard's wife Monie is also a genuine person. She has a sweet disposition and is very caring. Monie and I have several talks about life while I live with them. She always encourages me and is also supportive of me. I really appreciate the fact that she opened up her home to another woman. (I'm not sure whether or not most women would be so open). I worked with Bernard, but I had only met Monie (pronounced Mon-ee) maybe one time several years ago prior to moving in with them. Bernard and Monie's willingness to let me into their home and make me part of their family demonstrates so much about their character. Their children also welcomed me and made me feel like I was part of the family.

When I get home, I am greeted by 3 adorable little puppies. They are a mix of Pomeranian and Chihuahua. I call them "The Pups" because they move in unison and bark at me as their way of saying hello and welcome. I am exhausted from the flight and all of the emotion built up into moving back home. Later on that night a few former friends and co-workers come over for dinner. I will never be able to thank Bernard and Monie for everything they did for me. They opened up their beautiful home and allowed me to get myself together. Living with them is like living in the familiar family environment with my parents. They are my angels. I always pray that God continues to bless them. I spend the next few days and weeks reconnecting with my network of friends and professional colleagues.

I spend time thinking about my career and what type of work I would like to do. A lead comes through for me to work at a local domestic violence agency. I am very nervous during the interview, because I have never worked in that type of setting, and I am not sure if my professional background is what they are looking for. I have a Bachelor of Science degree in Business Administration, and now an MBA. But I have a passion for serving women who are dealing with Domestic Violence. My passion along with my experience as a Life Coach lands me the job. It's definitely not a high paying job, and there aren't a lot of hours, but I am doing work that I really love.

I am a Program Coordinator/Life Coach for clients living in our Safe House. My role has evolved into creating coaching programs for the clients and giving them the tools that they need to start their new life . And in all irony, I start my job on my birthday! What a great gift from God.

Another big gift arrived on 9/21/11. I was out at a networking event during the Congressional Black Caucus' (CBC) Annual Legislative Weekend in Washington, DC. Going anywhere by myself is a huge step now, because I still live with fear of doing things alone. It's not a crippling fear, but it does come up from time to time. As I walk around the event, I run into a guy who is there representing his own company. He seems really nice, so we start talking. His name is Brian, and he exudes confidence, but not in an arrogant way. He has a bright and genuine smile. I don't think too much of it at the time, but something feels very safe and familiar about him.

He asks me my name and I tell him, "my name is Soyini." "That's a beautiful name, what does it mean?, he inquires. "It means Rich Girl," I respond, noticing his mannerisms and his responses to what I am saying. "I like that," he says, "how do you spell it?" I spell it really slowly, but not so slow that he thinks I'm trying to be funny, "S-O-Y-I-N-I." As I spell it, I can tell that he is etching it in his memory. We talk for a moment and he gives me his card. I told him that I just moved back to the area and he offered to connect me with people who might be able to help me in my career search. I hold on to his card, but I didn't reach out to him like I said I would. I realized that I didn't give him any of my contact information either.

But as fate would have it, I actually RSVP'd for the event. (Something that I usually don't do, but something had told me to RSVP this time.) About a week after meeting Brian, I received an email from him. I was surprised and very happy, because I had a good feeling about him. We exchanged several emails over the next few days and talked on the phone a few times. He asked me if I would like to get together for dinner. I was on my way to Atlanta for an MBA conference, and I told him that we could get together after I return to Maryland a few days later.

We had our first date on 10/15/11. During our dinner date,

the conversation flowed and everything was so natural. I asked him, "so how did you get my email address?" He told me that he got a copy of the RSVP list because his company had co-sponsored the event, and he found my unique name on the list. He said he knew that he wanted to talk to me again after meeting me. Wow, I thought to myself. That was very thoughtful. We talked for hours during our date and I could tell that we both felt something really special.

After a few short weeks of dating, I knew that Brian was the one for me. We both felt it! I had never felt so happy and fulfilled in a relationship in my life. The timing was right, and we were both ready.

After a few months of being back East, I knew that I loved my job at the Domestic Violence Center of Howard County. It was truly the best job I ever had. I loved affecting the women's lives so directly. I loved watching them grow and seeing their tears and frowns turn into smiles and hope. I received so much healing working with them. I was so inspired by them. I loved creating coaching programs for them. I couldn't have designed a better job for myself. It broke my heart, when I had to make the decision to leave. I simply wasn't making enough money to live on my own there. After lots of conversation with God and myself, I knew that I had to leave and make more money somewhere else.

With tears in my eyes, I left the agency and began working for another company in a sales role. The job wasn't necessarily fulfilling or as enjoyable, but I was able to earn enough money to move out on my own. I learned new skills and met new people. The move also gave me more time to work on my own business as a life coach and wellness coach for companies. I was able to move back into my own home, that I used to perceive as a crime scene, the moment was surreal. I sat on the stairs near my living room and just thanked God.

My life had come in full circle. Here I was almost 3 years later after surviving 1/14/09 and I was back in my home, working, and dating the love of my life. Everything that I went through was worth it. I was experiencing a real happiness grounded in my new truth.

On February 9, 2013 Brian invited me to a dinner with his parents to celebrate their wedding anniversary. Their anniversary party had been held in December, but since I was working the day of the event, we decided to take them out to dinner at B. Smith's Restaurant in Washington DC's historic Union Station. I noticed that he had reserved a private room for us at the restaurant. I noticed that he seemed a little nervous, but it made sense, because he was planning the dinner for his parents. After a few moments, as other guests began to arrive, I started to see several of my friends, his friends, and then my brother! Hey, he lives in Philadelphia, what is he doing here? Then it hit me, this is for me. Brian dropped down to his knee and he said something to me. People were taking pictures and my brother had Skyped my parents in so they could see what was going on. Brian proposed, and I said YES!!!!! (After saying Oh My God, Oh My God, like 50 million times.)

On June 15, 2013 Brian and I were married. We had been talking about a wedding before we got engaged, and had started looking for venues to host our special day. Our wedding day was beautiful!! All the people who we love and care about were there to celebrate with us. It was a day that will never forget. As I said my vows to Brian, I knew that I meant every word. When my father walked me down the aisle, I started crying. I watched the genuine joy and happiness in the eyes of our family and friends. My dream of marrying my true love was happening in this moment.

After our wedding, we waited a couple of weeks before

heading to our honeymoon at Montego Bay in Jamaica. Sitting on the beach, soaking up the sun, I am so thankful for everything. My husband is a wonderful man, and my best friend. I am so happy and grateful for everything. Things have happened so fast, but everything has been right on time. God is great!

And now the next chapter in our life. Our baby will be here in Spring 2014. Everything that I wanted is happening. I am thankful for being given the chance to recreate my life. My new beginning is the best ever. Life is amazing!!

Q&A with Family and Friends

Mom

1) How long have you known Soyini?

I have known Soyini since she was born. From the minute I met her we bonded .This is due to the fact that she is my daughter. As such we have one of the most beautiful relationship you could imagine. We have great respect and love for each other. Our relationship will be solid for a life time.

2) How did you hear the news about 1/14/09?

On January 14, 2009 I received a phone call about 8:30 PM Pacific Standard time. I had just gotten home from work after having stopped at an open house for Wal-Mart. It was a fairly pleasant evening until the phone rang and the person on the phone introduced himself to me as a detective from the Laurel Maryland Police Department. He wanted to speak to Soyini Taylor's mother. After I answered he gave me the bad news. My life was changed forever. My one and only daughter had been shot and was being taken to the Trauma Center in Baltimore Maryland-- only if her condition could be stabilized. The medical team was working hard to stabilize her and would keep us informed of her status. At this point-- since she was not stable-- we didn't know if she would live or die. We were devastated; the entire event was surreal.

3) What was your initial response? (Physical, emotional, spiritual etc.)

When something like this happens it takes you by surprise you can't believe that it's happening in your very own family. Usually you see these things on CNN or in the movies -- not in your very own family. The incident has heightened my awareness of how others must suffer when they have this type of experience in their live. The crimes that are committed against others are now personal to me.

4) How if at all did it affect the way you view life?

After the incident I realized that you really never know what a person is capable of doing if he feels rejected or threatened. From this event, I learned that some will walk away while others might take drastic actions to solve a problematic relationship. You must be careful when choosing people to be a part of your life. My view of life has changed to the extent that all people in my life must earn my trust.

5) What is your advice for someone who might be going through a similar experience?

A person going through a similar situation should make the positive decision to separate from an abusive person before their life is altered forever. The wise thing to do is never stay too long with a person like this because the end result is always devastating. Since it is impossible to prevail with a person who has these types of tendencies it is best to leave them. Don't let them make you a victim.

Dad

1)   How long have you known Soyini?

I have known her all her life. Soyini is my first born and my only daughter. We have always had a good relationship. Soyini has always been well mannered. She always respected her peers and everyone else in the neighborhood. She has always been easy to get along with and very understanding.

2)   How did you hear the news about 1/14/09?

I was coming home from the mall with my wife. A few days prior to January 14, 2009, I had a feeling that something was going to happen. I didn't know how severe it would be, but I knew that something was going to happen soon.

When my wife and I got home, we received a call from the Detective alerting us of what happened. It was hard to take. I knew that things like this happen, but I didn't expect for it to hit home.

3)   What was your initial response? (Physical, emotional, spiritual etc.)

My first thought was that we had to get a flight out. I knew that we had to be in Maryland; there wasn't anything we could do in California. It was night time when we got the news, so we were able to get the first flight out of San Francisco the following morning.

When we arrived to the hospital, I didn't recognize my daughter. She was 3 times bigger than her normal size and all I could see were her eyes.

I kept asking the doctor if this was "Soyini Taylor" because she didn't look anything like herself.

4)   How if at all did it affect the way you view life?

I have a completely different view of life now. I have always been family oriented, but the experience increased my belief in the power of family. I have noticed that I am also a lot more concerned and caring about other people.

5)   What is your advice for someone who might be going through a similar experience?

The most important piece of advice is to "Have God in Your Heart." With God in your heart, you have to pray for the best. I have learned that there are many men out there who are capable of carrying out that type of attack. I would encourage young ladies in particular to be very careful when dating.

Also, the world is a more violent and dangerous place now than it was when I was growing up. Be careful who you talk to and who you associate with.

Dwayne - Younger Brother

1)   How long have you known Soyini?

I am her Oldest Brother, so I have known her all my life

2)   How did you hear the news about 1/14/09?

I was sleeping at my then girlfriends' (now wife) house when my mother called my girlfriends' cell phone at approximately 4am EST. My mother couldn't reach me on my cell phone because the battery was dead, so she called Carla. It was without a doubt the worst news I had ever received in my life!

3)   What was your initial response? (Physical, emotional, spiritual etc.)

My initial response was that I must be having a nightmare because something like this couldn't have happened to someone in my family. This was the most difficult situation I had to deal with in my life for several reasons. First of all, I didn't know if Soyini was going to survive the assault and I didn't know if the accuser was still on the prowl. Secondly, I thought my sister can't be taken away from me already, she has too much life to live! My third response was whether my family would be able to emotionally get through this tragedy. I knew I would be able to handle it (though arduous) but it would take some time to overcome such a malicious act towards human life.

4)   How if at all did it affect the way you view life?

My views towards life have changed! As I reflect on the courage and unflagging determination my sister exhibited during the attack and her recovery, I am at a loss for words. It is mind-boggling as to how mentally and physically strong she is! I told myself that she is a true champion! If you ever wonder what it is like to stand-up and tackle adversity by the horns, you need to speak with her because she can provide a detailed testimonial for when giving up isn't an option! I told myself from that day forward that the mind truly controls the body!

All the days I spent at the hospital while helping Soyini regain her vigor, I could only think about how I should never complain about being tired! I always remind myself, Soyini never fatigued nor quit so why should I! That statement helps me get through the day and continue to keep kicking and pushing and striving for greatness. We can truly do anything we believe! Soyini is living proof of that!

Furthermore, life is precious and be thankful for each and everyday you have with the people you love. Perpetuate a state of positivity in all your relationships!

5)What is your advice for someone who might be going through a similar experience?

Focus on the positive and don't give the negative energy any attention.

Eric - Youngest Brother

1) How long have you known Soyini?

Soyini has known me ever since the day I was born. She is the only sister I have and the eldest of the Taylor children.

2) How did you hear the news about 1/14/09?

I heard about the tragic news of the event that occurred on 1/14/09 from my parents. My parents called me because I was living in Minnesota at the time. When they told me about what happen I felt my heart sink into my stomach.

3)   What was your initial response? (Physical, emotional, spiritual etc.)

I was in a state of disbelief. I had a long conversation with my sister the previous day. We had a ritual of speaking to each other at least once a week to discuss things that were going on in our lives. This conversation stuck out to me in particular because my sister had been volunteering on, then Senator Barack Obama's, campaign to be elected president. My sister was excited about volunteering on the campaign and I loved to hear her talk about it. During this conversation I could also sense a tone of sadness in Soyini's voice. I believe that my sister intuited that something ominous was going to take place but she did not want to tell me because she knew I would worry about her.

4)   How if at all did it affect the way you view life?

It had a profound impact on the way I view life. This event showed me how precious a human life is; you can literally be here today and gone tomorrow. I have vicariously learned the importance forgiveness through my sister. I admire how my sister did not allow one person to destroy her spirit or take away her happiness. I see my sister as a walking miracle!

5)   What is your advice for someone who might be going through a similar experience?

If you are involved with a person like the individual that my sister was you must get away from them because you never know what an individual is capable of.

Tonia - Friend

1.   How long have you known Soyini?

I met Soyini my sophomore year of college at Bowie State

University. She was visiting from California on an exchange program. We were both about 19 years old and had instant chemistry as friends, the kind you should have, that doesn't require much work. That has always been the nature of our friendship, since we're both easy going and friendly at heart, we had that in common. We spent time together ever since, going to parties and taking road trips, shopping in NYC. We truly enjoyed our 20's together traveling to Paris and South Beach. What a blast!! I have memories that mean so much to me and have added so much to my life because of Soyini, and I am grateful for that.

2.   How did you hear the news about 1/14/09?

The news about 1/14/09 in my mind still feels like yesterday. It's visceral even now when I recall that first phone call. I was in my bedroom, early in the morning with my husband. I re-member I was about to walk to him to the front door when I saw Dre's (Andrea) number come up on my phone. I thought it was strange because she didn't call me that often, she usual-ly text me. Even then in light of all I knew Soyini was going through with her ex-boyfriend, it still hadn't occurred to me that something was wrong. Until, she said the words "Tonia, I'm so sorry to have to tell you this, but Soyini has been shot." I think I instantly dropped the phone; I was in shock and my husband Markie turned to look at me. I somehow got the phone in my hand and I mumbled a few words to Andrea asking what she meant and where was Soyini? She managed to explain that he shot Soyini and they weren't sure if she was dead. They couldn't find the information on the news or Inter-net. Looking back now, I feel none of us wanted to know, so researching was not the priority at the time. As I said, Markie was there with me so he looked up a few things, made some calls, and didn't want to worry with me with what he found. I remember rushing to put on some clothes and driving from

Delaware to the hospital in Baltimore. It was a real blur at that point. All I wanted was to make sure my friend was ok, and if I could just see her with my own eyes, everything would be alright.

3.   What was your initial response? (Physical, emotional, spiritual etc.)

I felt stupid and regretful all at the same time. I was wrecked with grief and that was too much to bare so I immediately went to analyzing and trying to make sense of it all. I couldn't wrap my head around it being true. All his crazy actions, and reckless behavior, I still didn't think he would hurt her this way. I was confused on how something like this could happen. In my mind, I'd never known such a horrendous act of cowardice and sickeningly brutal behavior. I couldn't make the connection on how Soyini's life was touched by such violence. It would be as if it were me and I thought this could truly happen to anyone. I was sick, and sad, and mute. I cried for awhile but then had no tears left. It takes a lot for me to cry and I am more prone to anger before tears but I was trying to survive it and make some sense of everything. So, I prayed for Soyini's peace of mind, that she wasn't afraid anymore, that she be safe and rest in God's embrace.

4.   How if at all did it affect the way you view life?

I have been a spiritual person all my life. From religion to spirituality to religion again, and now some combination of both. So inherently, I knew God was at work. I knew there was a plan for her, for all of us who knew her in some way. I often think of the world as a big picture on a map (God's view I like to think), and for it to make sense to me I imagine many red points all over the map that must be connected in order to arrive at a certain place on the map. Now, all points will not be beautiful, all locations will not be easy to travel through, there will be valleys, and sunsets, and rain in great abundance some days, some years, but this is all necessary to arrive the way were intended to arrive. There are certain things in you that God wants to see strengthened and some things weakened or lessened in us. He sees the road from beginning to end and worries not for the bumps along the way. So I knew, without a single doubt, that Soyini was going to be better for this, that her life would be complete in some way; full of depth and a generosity of spirit that I knew she needed to make it through. So, I was not surprised when she did :-)

5.   What is your advice for someone who might be going through a similar experience?

As for advice, that's tough since I was a witness, and not a survivor myself. But, as a witness to it all, I know there were things Soyini wishes she would have done differently and those are the things I would caution others to heed. Intuition being the most important to me. If you have a feeling something is not right, not quite safe, about a person, listen to that feeling. Do your research, meet a man's family to see where he comes from and who he learned from as well. Watch for signs of alcohol or drug abuse, that some people use as coping mechanisms for sometimes very serious issues. Offer outside assistance to them, but most importantly GET OUT!!!! The other side of that would be what Soyini did. She stayed strong, she knew she was a true survivor, that if she could conquer this, then she could make it through anything. She depended on the love of family and friends which is a huge support for her and you need that. You cannot do it alone. What impressed me the most about Soyini was her willingness to share her story. Every time she told her story, I feel she got a little bit stronger each time. It was cleansing for her spirit and reenergizing as well. This was motivation for her, I think she wanted to make others around her proud, but even more so she wanted to make herself proud. She accomplished that and much more.

Jennie - Friend

1) How long have you known Soyini?

I met Soyini in 2000/2001. She was among the first people I met when I moved to Maryland from Colorado. We went to school together at Inner Visions Worldwide which provided a unique connection for us, as the full focus of that program was on personal/spiritual development. We also had the unique connection that we both loved the West Coast (she's from Oakland, CA, I moved to the East Coast from Colorado) but we both had this draw to the East Coast and had relocated out here and started our lives again here.

Soyini has become one of my dearest friends over the years. We have a unique relationship in that we don't see each other much but we both know that if we need anything, the other will be available and will be there without question. We have the kind of friendship that we can pick up the phone and re-connect at any point. We can/do talk freely with each other in support of the other. Over the years, she has also introduced me to some close friends of hers, and a couple of them have become dear friends of mine too. Soyini is someone that I anticipate I will stay uniquely connected to throughout the rest of my life.

2) How did you hear the news about 1/14/09?

I heard the news about 01/14/09 from my colorist/hairdresser. Soyini and I go to the same hair salon and my hairdresser knew of our friendship.

I was getting my hair done in preparation for the inauguration ceremonies for President Barack Obama. I had just talked to Soyini a few days before this happened, and we'd just exchanged emails a day or two before this event to confirm that we would both be at the training and to learn where we would both be stationed on the Mall – we were both scheduled to be volunteers for the Official Inauguration Ceremony.

3)   What was your initial response? (Physical, emotional, spiritual etc.)

I was talking with my colorist (Michelle) and I was none-the-wiser about what happened the night before with Soyini. I was excited about the coming events and yapping it up with Michelle and some others in the salon.

After about twenty to thirty minutes, when the other ladies had gone off to their respective stations, Michelle looked into the mirror and stared straight into my eyes. The emotion of the moment went quickly from light and excited to grounded and serious. I knew something was wrong, but I had no idea what was to come. Michelle looked at me and said, "You haven't heard the news, have you?"

My heart sank. I knew something awful happened, and while Michelle and I knew some mutual people at the salon, I knew it had nothing to do with anyone at the salon – the spirit there was too high and happy to have the news involve with any-one immediately at the salon. I remember feeling immediate-ly light-headed and prepared to hear the worst. I attribute that dramatic shift from coming from a feeling of high/excitement to feeling like someone had just punched me and took my breath away – it was such a strong shift in direction of emo-tion. Thankfully, because there were so many people gathered and talking when I first arrived (everyone was excited about the upcoming Inauguration for Barack Obama), Michelle had held this close to her chest until she could tell me in a sup-portive manner, without anyone else around.

Michelle said, "I could tell by the way you came in here today that you hadn't heard yet, but I didn't want to share this with you with the other ladies around. It's about your friend Soyini. She was shot last night. Her boyfriend shot her. It happened at her house… you live by her, right? It happened late at night. The police caught him – evidently the boyfriend is dead. I just happened to read the Laurel news online and I saw the news this morning."

Michelle didn't say what happened to Soyini. I was in shock. I sat there completely still and speechless. I did not know what to say or how to feel. I was scared to ask if my friend survived. Somehow it didn't sink in that he was dead yet – and I was still scared he might be "out there" or at the hospital and able to come back and stalk her again.

I took a few deep breaths and forced myself at ask, "Michelle, did she die? Do you know?"

Michelle grabbed my shoulders and provided support while I sat in the chair in shock, "Girl, I don't know how she's doing, but from what I understand she survived. She's at the hospital." Tears started falling out of my eyes uncontrollably and yet I still felt oddly emotionally disconnected – I had so many conflicting emotions coming to the surface at once that I couldn't really tell what I was feeling. I was relieved she to learn that she was alive and yet terrified to learn the details about the situation (e.g. how/where she was shot, how many times she was shot, and the ultimate outcome on her physical/ mental/emotional well-being). And just because she was alive now, I didn't know the details of the situation and didn't know if she would survive. Again, I just felt shock. I don't know that I've ever felt shock or stunned like that before in my life. It was very surreal.

I recall Michelle saying that she tried to find out more details but that she that there wasn't more information than that online. Michelle had only shared the news with the stylist at the shop that did Soyini's hair, and she [the stylist] didn't know anything else either. Michelle shared that she would have expected Soyini would be at University of Maryland's Shock/Trauma Center given the circumstances. I remember Michelle offering as much information and support as she could for the first few minutes (which felt like one very long moment in time that was almost timeless... everything came to a stop around me).

I don't remember much of what she said after that. I remember that I kept focusing on my breathing and that tears just kept coming out of my eyes. I remember that there was one woman under the dryer next to my station who had a clear look of concern and confusion on her face – she'd just seen me happy and joy-filled to "this." I remember that moment because it felt very slow-motion too. She asked me if I was okay. I couldn't respond. I just looked at her – Michelle quietly told the woman what happened, "her girlfriend was shot by her boyfriend last night." She said it so calmly and to not draw attention to our corner of the salon. The woman immediately provided solace, and she asked, too, if Soyini had survived. But, before I knew it I had a few women around me providing me support anyway (again, there was so much excitement in the salon I would guess we attracted attention because of the dramatic shift in our spirits/conversation).

I do remember how much I appreciated how respectful they were being of the circumstances – I recall concern for Soyini and less questions about the details about what happened. I remember a couple of the women giving me hugs, a couple praying, and them immediately going back to what they were doing to give me space. I remember a few others in the salon asking them what was going on (I could see what was going on behind me in the mirror) and what I noticed at first was that they were saying "she's okay" and just going on with everything like it was nothing. I appreciated that greatly – I already felt overwhelmed, and I tend to take a moment to adjust to my emotions/circumstances and to let things sink in – I really only wanted to be by Michelle and the woman who was near me drying her hair.

I remember we all sat in silence for a few minutes after that. I remember my brain being flooded with thoughts and then seemingly going blank, over and over again. I remember asking Michelle blankly, "what do I do?" I remember feeling helpless at that moment. I had no idea how to find out where she was – at least not a first. I felt weird reaching out to her girlfriends because we'd just started to build relationships with each other, but I knew I needed to reach out and let them know and/or connect with them. Most of all, I realized all I could do was pray at that point. I knew this situation was in God's hands and I remember feeling completely at His mercy. I felt helpless, relieved (that he was dead and that this whole situation was "over") but also tentative about Soyini's condition. Somehow though I knew in my heart she was going to be alright. I felt like since she survived, she just had to be okay.

The next major point I remember is Michelle reminding me again that he was dead. When I fully took that fact in, then I really felt relieved. I did not want him dead out of vengeance – I was relieved because he was so unstable in the months leading up to this I did not think he would stop pursuing her until they were both dead. I had a brief thought that had he stayed alive, that he would just continue to pursue her for the rest of his life. From my perspective, he was such a tortured soul and he was so obsessed with pursuing her, that I felt huge sense of relief that should Soyini survive, that she could have her life back.

After I processed all those emotions, I was relieved he was dead, glad she survived, and eager to find out her current state. Somehow I knew she was going to be alright.

4) How if at all did it affect the way you view life?

I don't know that it's had a huge effect on the way I view life. I would say that this situation, along with some personal circumstances of my own with people close to me with emotional issues, has made me more firm about how I manage my own communications and interactions with those who have emotional issues or who are in emotional distress. I would say that it has me even more thoughtful in those interactions. It has me even more aware and more prayerful when I come across individuals who are clearly going through something, and yet it has me even more capable to (if not adamant about) "love from a distance."

This situation (again, along with other circumstances in my own life) has made me even more aware of well-meaning, but enabling behaviors, that I might have even had with those under emotional distress. It's been a reminder that I need to steer away from those old habits – I now more consciously and thoughtfully replace those old responses with empathy and support, but I don't take on those individual's issues. I realize people in that kind of pain are capable of working through their issues – if they choose to. Being firm with them about my boundaries is essential. Ironically I think this situation has helped me be even more adamant about supporting others to support themselves, and it has made me less willing, able, or even available, to support others going through emotional distress and who are not taking responsibility for themselves.

As a single woman who is actively dating, I admit that this has had an impact on me to be even more cautious about inviting anyone that I'm dating to my personal home, or into my life, period. I've been actively dating again for about the last year, and I have only allowed one person to my home that I've dated. This is partly due to my protecting my own private space – but I'd be lying if I didn't acknowledge that this situation with Soyini hasn't made me even more cautious about opening up my life/world to a potential life partner. I'm adamant about seeking out and inviting in only those who are "emotionally healthy" – I don't mean emotionally perfect, but responsible, self-aware, and personally accountable. I remember how frustrating it was to watch how helpless Soyini was in trying to keep him away from her, e.g. how he pushed the boundaries of the restraining order and how he was following her. She had no peace of mind and no safe space until he was finally gone. I certainly communicate clearer with anyone I come across that expresses any significant dysfunction (particularly around control and/or obsessive behavior) – I'm much more sensitive to individuals in situations that could be dangerous.

5)   What is your advice for someone who might be going through a similar experience?

Obviously every situation is unique, but these are things that come to mind if I knew someone else going through a similar situation.

First and foremost – do not isolate yourself. Reach out to your friends – your support network – to support you out of this situation and back to a peaceful life. Be open and candid with those in your support network that you know will be grounded and provide prayerful, insightful, and educated guidance – focusing on real solutions and not the problem (e.g. no talking up the drama… but only talking up the solutions and supporting the friend through the circumstances).

(1) Acknowledge that the person is not well, and acknowledge that it is not your responsibility to fix them. (2) Be empathetic. (3) Have absolute, clear boundaries. (4) Be firm in communications and actions – keep communications short, clear, concise and with a goal of completely disconnecting from that person. If you don't know how to do this when the situation is occurring, FIND SOMEONE ASAP to coach you and follow their instruction until you learn how to communication with clear boundaries. I think all too frequently (5) Have an emotionally mature support network to support you in navigating circumstances (how you communicate with them and what actions you take) to keep you safe. (6) Seek out professionals that deal with these extreme circumstances for options on how to keep safe, and how to disengage from this person. (7) Don't point fingers – at yourself or the ill person – there is no power in blaming or judging yourself or the other person. Simply acknowledge that things aren't right and take action to keep yourself (and your loved ones) safe from harm. (8) Take legal action where/if necessary. Realize that even legal actions can't/won't necessarily control the person – and you cannot control another person – so be extra diligent about taking proactive action on your behalf to be aware and keep yourself safe. (9) If the person does escalate to the point that they invade your personal space or escalate to the point of threating bodily harm, remain calm, focused, prayerful and DO NOT let the person isolate you… fight back… your life depends on it. (10) Don't look back – and don't drudge up the past – especially if the person remains alive (which was not what happened with this situation). Let the person go. Communicating or engaging with any aspect of them and their lives will only keep the energy going. Let them go so they can (hopefully) take their attention somewhere else. (11) Be persistent with all this – some people are so emotionally distressed this will take months (years?) to break the cycle. You can only control you. Be

prayerful, calm, confident, and self-assured so that you can be open to the daily steps to guide you through this and back to a peaceful life again.

Charisse - Friend

1) How long have you known Soyini?

I have known Soyini aka So-So since Fall (maybe October) 2000. We met at Xerox in Washington D.C.

So-So is a very close friend, she is like my little sister.

2) How did you hear the news about 1/14/09?

I was leaving the Sports and Learning Center in Landover, MD and I received a phone call from Andrea aka Dre Dre informing me that she had received news that So-So had been shot but she was unable to contact So-So's parents or get anyone to confirm the news. Dre Dre discussed the information she had and then devised a plan to contact So-So's parents. We weren't for certain if they knew or even if the information we had was accurate. After a bunch of confusion, gathering additional information, we found out that the tragic news about our friend was accurate and where she was. In route to the hospital, we were not certain about So-So's condition. Was my friend/sister alive or dead?

3) What was your initial response? (Physical, emotional, spiritual etc.)

When I received the news from Dre Dre that So-So had been shot, I was partially in shock if that makes sense. I say partially because my immediate thought was "he got her before she got him and I thought something like this would occur after the court date." I cried and asked God to let my friend be alive. I was mad that this situation of stalking had become tragic and I knew it would end either So-So being hurt/killed or him. So-So and I had a conversation about stalkers, some behaviors of those that have psychological turmoil from rejection and abandonment. I wanted to get to the hospital asap and let my friend/sis know that I was there and she was not alone. I was angry at the police for not being able to do more to protect my friend. The pain that I felt for her parents was overwhelming for me. Yes, I was in pain and scared as I did not want to lose my friend, but I could not imagine the range and intensity of emotions her parents were experiencing. This was their oldest child, baby girl. They had to travel from one coast to another not knowing their daughter's future. After the immediate response to the news and crying, I told myself in order to help So-So and our friends, and remain a level head; I had to look at So-So as a patient. This emotional strategy helped me to be there for others who loved So-So and was afraid of the situation. Although I held it together while we were at the hospital, when I went home I released all emotions and continued to pray for my friend, her family, our friends, and my strength to be the support that So-So and others needed.

4)   How if at all did it affect the way you view life?

My view on life did not really alter that much. I know that we can be here in one minute and gone the next, as well as life is not fair, and we have a lot of dangerous and mentally unstable people in our society, and at times, our immediate environment. I understood the negative outcomes of a stalking situation from previously counseling patients in similar situations. It was my experience as a therapist that I was able to have the most difficult conversation that I have had to have with a friend/sister. I am thankful that God used me to pour some wisdom into So-So through my experiences secondary to those of previous patients. I had to tell my friend that this situation would come down to her or his life (his or her death). When So-So asked "Risse would you go back home… should I go back to my house?" I told So-So I would go home because I would not want to run from him the remainder of my life. I told her he would follow her/track her down and continue to bother her family. I advised her to inform family and friends and those around her to make sure people in her life knew what was happening. My friend/sister took my advice and lived in fear every day. It saddened and hurt me to hear what she had to deal with on a daily basis. I am so proud of So-So for trusting in God and conquering her fear. It was not easy advice to give and I know it was not easy to make the decision to return home and live her life in fear of what this mentally ill man will do.

5)   What is your advice for someone who might be going through a similar experience?

You don't have to tell everyone your business, but have that friend or family member that you trust to be honest with you about people in your life. Be mindful of others behaviors. Don't be embarrassed or ashamed about negative behaviors that someone else can demonstrate to you. Although the laws for protecting victims of stalkers need improvement continue to file peace orders…continue to have a paper trail of your complaint. Let neighbors, family, friends, associates, etc. know what is happening to you and provide as much information about the perpetrator as possible. These things helped save Soyini's life. Most importantly, do not confuse obsession, controlling behaviors as love. Mental illness is not always visible like a physical injury. I always say that there is a fine line between sanity and insanity. Humans have different coping skills level. Our greatest protection is having a relationship with God and having faith in him. Lean on other strong, positive, and loving people to help you when you feel you don't have the strength to help yourself.

Andrea - Friend

1.   How long have you known Soyini?

I have known Soyini since 1999, maybe even 1998. Wow, 14 -15 years!!!

2.   How did you hear the news about 1/14/09?

A friend from work saw a news report on television and called me a bit before 9am. She called me and asked if I had talked to Soyini - which I found to be an odd question at that particular hour. She was very careful not to alarm me but mentioned the news report gently. At that moment I had never felt so much fear for the truth, ever.

3.   What was your initial response? (Physical, emotional, spiritual etc.)

Disbelief. Denial. I was determined to prove it wasn't my friend. I called her phone begging God that she would pick up. She didn't. I Googled it. I saw the article...and her address On ABC.com. My heart sank.

4.   How if at all did it affect the way you view life?

This incident taught me several truths. That life can be absolutely cruel. That in spite of the cruelty, God's heart will replace mine when it's broken. That His angels surround me at all times but I may not be able to see that because of the pain. That without faith, there is indeed death. Death of mind, body and spirit. Soyini showed me that life is to be LIVED. To soar as high as you can for as long as you can. To push back and fight for the life you want. You can have it.

5.   What is your advice for someone who might be going through a similar experience?

My advice: Love yourself and understand your self-worth.

Don't allow the first look (or second for that matter) to determine your reaction to life. Forgive so your heart can be free. Be smart and use God's eyes as your guide. You will not fail and you WILL live with joy.

Yvonne - Friend

1) How long have you known Soyini?

Soyini is my best friend. I have known her since I was 12 years old.

2) How did you hear the news about 1/14/09?

My cousin Lisa called me on a Thursday Evening. I was excited about all of our plans for The Big Inauguration Weekend in DC. When I answered the phone, I said, "what's up cousin!" Lisa replied with a very low and somber tone, she said," It's Soyini." I felt my heart sink into my shoes, I knew it was bad news. My cousin mumbled, "she was shot" and I drowned out the rest of what followed.

3) What was your initial response? (Physical, emotional, spiritual etc.)

My knees buckled and I dropped to the icy cold cement, and screamed out loud. Thoughts were racing through my mind, my best friend is dead, my best friend is dead, I can't believe that God would allow this to happen to Soyini, I can't believe that my best friend is gone. Then I heard my cousin mumble "she's in the hospital". All of a sudden, I was able to regain my composure, "she is alive." I knew that God spared her life for a reason.

4) How if at all did it affect the way you view life?

Soyini's experience has taught me that God can bring tragedy and adversity and our lives to test our will and faith. In Soyini's case, I feel that God gave her a testimony. She has inspired me with her strength, fortitude and determination. Soyini, could have thrown in the towel and given up on life instead she strengthened her faith in God, and persevered through very painful and tough times.

5) What is your advice for someone who might be going through a similar experience?

Sometimes, God may bring tragedy and adversity into our lives to test our will and faith. God never brings any situation into our lives that we cannot endure. So when you are faced with adversity, the best thing you can do is armor yourself with your faith and belief in God, he will make a way.

<u>Appendix and Resources</u>

What is Domestic Violence ?

According to the United States Depart of Justice Office on Violence Against Women March 2013, Domestic Violence is defined as a pattern of abusive behavior in any relationship that is used by one partner to gain or maintain power and control over another intimate partner. Domestic violence can be physical, sexual, emotional, economic, or psychological actions or threats of actions that influence another person. This includes any behaviors that intimidate, manipulate, humiliate, isolate, frighten, terrorize, coerce, threaten, blame, hurt, injure, or wound someone.

Physical Abuse: Hitting, slapping, shoving, grabbing, pinching, biting, hair pulling, etc. are types of physical abuse. This type of abuse also includes denying a partner medical care or forcing alcohol and/or drug use upon him or her.

Sexual Abuse: Coercing or attempting to coerce any sexual contact or behavior without consent. Sexual abuse includes, but is certainly not limited to, marital rape, attacks on sexual parts of the body, forcing sex after physical violence has occurred, or treating one in a sexually demeaning manner.

Emotional Abuse: Undermining an individual's sense of self-worth and/or self-esteem is abusive. This may include, but is not limited to constant criticism, diminishing one's abilities, name-calling, or damaging one's relationship with his or her children.

Economic Abuse: Is defined as making or attempting to make an individual financially dependent by maintaining total control over financial resources, withholding one's access to money, or forbidding one's attendance at school or employment.

Psychological Abuse: Elements of psychological abuse include - but are not limited to - causing fear by intimidation; threatening physical harm to self, partner, children, or partner's family or friends; destruction of pets and property; and forcing isolation from family, friends, or school and/or work.

Domestic violence can happen to anyone regardless of race, age, sexual orientation, religion, or gender. Domestic violence affects people of all socioeconomic backgrounds and education levels. Domestic violence occurs in both opposite-sex and same-sex relationships and can happen to intimate partners who are married, living together, or dating.

Domestic violence not only affects those who are abused, but also has a substantial effect on family members, friends, co-workers, other witnesses, and the community at large. Children, who grow up witnessing domestic violence, are among those seriously affected by this crime. Frequent exposure to violence in the home not only predisposes children to numerous social and physical problems, but also teaches them that violence is a normal way of life - therefore, increasing their risk of becoming society's next generation of victims and abusers.

Sources: National Domestic Violence Hotline, National Center for Victims of Crime, and WomensLaw.org.

Red Flags

Remember that every domestic violence case is different. Everyone doesn't see all of these signs, and also remember that many times it takes a while before the signs appear. The signs can be noticed during the honeymoon phase of dating or after the relationship is more mature. The most important thing is to listen to your intuition. Sometimes you know that something doesn't feel right, but you just can't your finger on it. Trust yourself; you are most likely feeling uneasy for a reason. The National Network to End Domestic Violence provided some of the signs/red flags on their website. I also included information from other domestic violence survivors that I talked to in support group settings.

1. Wants to move too quickly into the relationship.

2. Does not honor your boundaries.

3. Is excessively jealous and accuses you of having affairs.

4. Wants to know where you are all of the time and frequently calls, emails and texts you throughout the day.

5. Criticizes you or puts you down; most commonly tells you that you are "crazy," "stupid" and/or "fat," or that no one would ever want or love you.

6. Says one thing and does another.

7. Takes no responsibility for their behavior and blames others.

8. Has a history of battering.

9. Blames the entire failure of previous relationships on their partner; for example, "My ex was a total bitch."

10. Grew up in an abusive or violent home.

11. Insists that you stop spending time with your friends or family.

12. Seems "too good to be true."

13. Insists that you stop participating in leisure interests.

14. Rages out of control and is impulsive.

15. Always angry at someone or something

16.   Tell you how to dress or act

17.   Lie to you, don't show up for dates, disappears for days at a time

18.   Cheat on you or have lots of partners

19.   Nags or forces you to be sexual when you don't want to

20.   History of abusing siblings, other family members, children, or pets

21.   History of trouble with the law

22.   Physically rough with you (push, shove, pull, yank, squeeze, restrain)

23.   Try to isolate you and control who you see and/or where you go

24.   Don't listen to you or show interest in you opinions or feelings

25.   Blame all arguments and problems on you

26.   Threaten to commit suicide if you break up with him/her

27.   You feel afraid to bring up certain subjects because the other person will get mad

28.   Extreme mood swings…. I love you one minute and then tear you down the next minute

29.   You feel anxious and/or nervous around him/her

30.   You feel tied down like you have to check-in excessively

Power and Control Wheel

Domestic Violence is all about Power and Control. The Power and Control Wheel is used by many Domestic Violence Organizations to describe an abusive relationship. The first time that I saw this wheel, it made so much sense. Here is the Power and Control Wheel that the Domestic Violence Hotline uses.

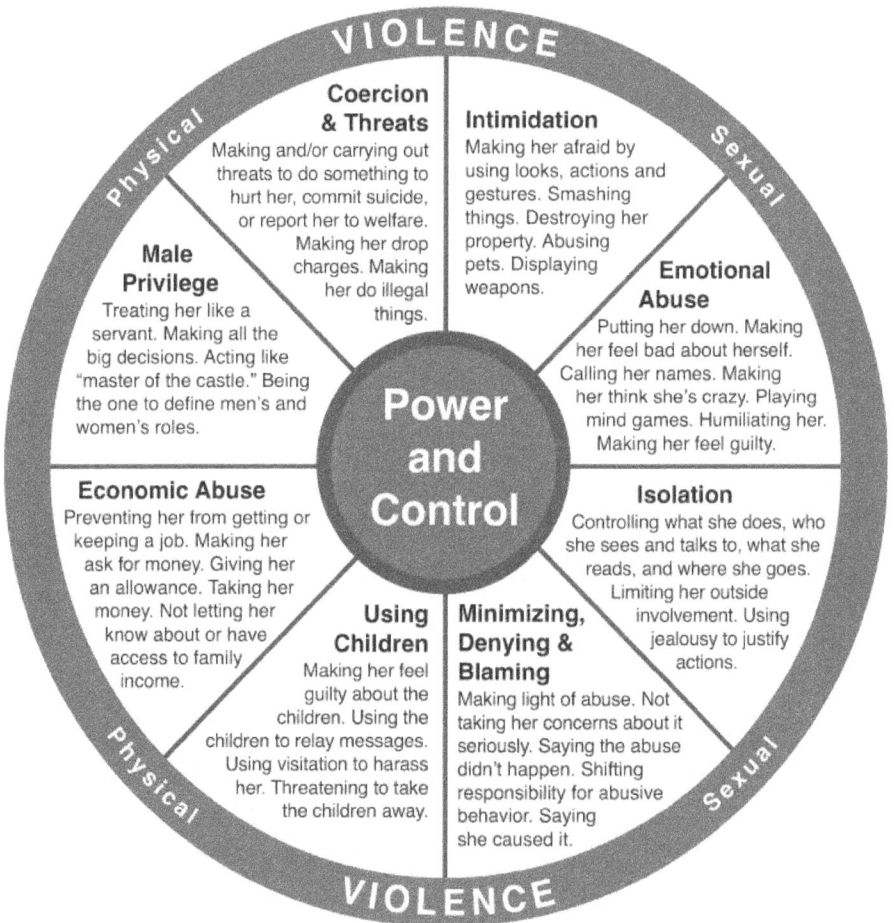

VIOLENCE

Physical

Sexual

Coercion & Threats
Making and/or carrying out threats to do something to hurt her, commit suicide, or report her to welfare. Making her drop charges. Making her do illegal things.

Intimidation
Making her afraid by using looks, actions and gestures. Smashing things. Destroying her property. Abusing pets. Displaying weapons.

Male Privilege
Treating her like a servant. Making all the big decisions. Acting like "master of the castle." Being the one to define men's and women's roles.

Emotional Abuse
Putting her down. Making her feel bad about herself. Calling her names. Making her think she's crazy. Playing mind games. Humiliating her. Making her feel guilty.

Power and Control

Economic Abuse
Preventing her from getting or keeping a job. Making her ask for money. Giving her an allowance. Taking her money. Not letting her know about or have access to family income.

Isolation
Controlling what she does, who she sees and talks to, what she reads, and where she goes. Limiting her outside involvement. Using jealousy to justify actions.

Using Children
Making her feel guilty about the children. Using the children to relay messages. Using visitation to harass her. Threatening to take the children away.

Minimizing, Denying & Blaming
Making light of abuse. Not taking her concerns about it seriously. Saying the abuse didn't happen. Shifting responsibility for abusive behavior. Saying she caused it.

Physical

Sexual

VIOLENCE

Getting Help

It's important for victims of Domestic Violence to know that they are not alone. There is a lot of free and confidential support for victims of domestic violence. I have listed a few National Domestic Violence Agencies in the United States. The national agencies are a great place to start, however, you should also find the local agencies in your area. The local agencies provide a number of services that are usually free. Some of the services offered are: counseling, advocacy and legal assistance, crisis intervention, housing, help for abusers, and survivor support.

1. National Coalition Against Domestic Violence

http://www.ncadv.org/

2. National Domestic Violence Hotline

http://www.thehotline.org/

3. National Network to End Domestic Violence☐

http://nnedv.org/

4. United States Department of Justice's Office on Violence Against Women (OVW)

http://www.ovw.usdoj.gov/

5. The National Center For Victims of Crime

http://www.victimsofcrime.org/

6. National Teen Dating Abuse Helpline

http://www.loveisrespect.org/

Technology Safety

Computers record everything you do on the internet, so you should think about ways to maintain your on line safety as you get assistance with Domestic Violence. Below are a few tips, but you can definitely see more of an exhaustive list from one of the national organizations listed above.

Computer Safety

If you are in danger use a computer that your abuser doesn't have access to or even remote (hacking) access. Try to use a computer in public library, internet café, work computer, domestic violence shelter or agency, or at a trusted friend or co workers house.

Email and Instant Messaging

This isn't the preferred way to seek help for domestic violence because your abuser may know how to get access to your account. Consider creating a new email account on a safer computer that your abuser doesn't have access to. Remember to avoid using too much personal detail in your personal information. Don't use any part of your real name in your email address.

Change Your User Names and Passwords

Create new usernames and passwords for your email, online banking, and other sensitive accounts. Even if you don't think your abuser has your passwords, he may have guessed or used a spyware or key logging program to get them. Choose passwords that your abuser can't guess (avoid birthdays, nicknames, and other personal information).

Phone Safety

The Help Guide.org has a very helpful resource section for Domestic Violence victims and support with phone and technology safety.

When seeking help for domestic violence, call from a public pay phone or another phone outside the house if possible. In the U.S., you can call 911 for free on most public phones, so know where the closest one is in case of emergency.

Avoid cordless telephones. If you're calling from your home, use a corded phone because it is more private, and less easy to tap.

Call collect or use a prepaid phone card. Remember that if you use your own home phone or telephone charge card, the phone numbers that you call will be listed on the monthly bill that is sent to your home. Even if you've already left by the time the bill arrives, your abuser may be able to track you down by the phone numbers you've called for help.

Check your cell phone settings. There are cell phone technologies your abuser can use to listen in on your calls or track your location.

Your abuser can use your cell phone as a tracking device if it has GPS, is in "silent mode," or is set to "auto answer." So consider turning it off when not in use or leaving it behind when fleeing your abuser.

Get your own cell phone. Consider purchasing a prepaid cell phone or another cell phone that your abuser doesn't know about. Some domestic violence shelters offer free cell phones to battered women. Call your local hotline to find out more.

Source: Help Guide.org

What is stalking?

The National Center for Victims of Crime has a wealth of information on stalking. http://www.victimsofcrime.org/

Be sure to download the Stalking Resources Guide.

Stalking

While legal definitions of stalking vary from one jurisdiction to another, a good working definition of stalking is a course of conduct directed at a specific person that would cause a reasonable person to feel fear.

Stalking is serious, often violent, and can escalate over time

Some things stalkers do:

1.   Follow you and show up wherever you are.

2.   Send unwanted gifts, letters, cards, or e-mails.

3.   Damage your home, car, or other property.

4.   Monitor your phone calls or computer use.

5.   Use technology, like hidden cameras or global positioning systems (GPS), to track where you go.

6.   Drive by or hang out at your home, school, or work.

7.   Threaten to hurt you, your family, friends, or pets.

8.   Find out about you by using public records or online search services, hiring investigators, going through your garbage, or contacting friends, family, neighbors, or co-workers.

9.   Posting information or spreading rumors about you on the Internet, in a public place, or by word of mouth.

10.   Other actions that control, track, or frighten you.

Source: The National Center for Victims of Crime http://www.victimsofcrime.org/

Safety Plan

Your safety is important. When you are in an abusive relationship it is difficult to think your way to safety. A safety plan is your first step to restoring your safety. The Domestic Violence Hotline defines what a safety plan is. A safety plan is a personalized, practical plan that includes ways to remain safe while in a relationship, planning to leave, or after you leave. Safety planning involves how to cope with emotions, tell friends and family about the abuse, take legal action and more. Safety Plans are designed to fit your unique situation. The Domestic Violence Hotline or your local domestic violence agency or shelter can help you with your planning. The planning can be for various living arrangements: Safety Planning with children, Safety while living with an abusive partner, Safety Planning with pets or Safety Planning while pregnant.

This is the most crucial step to ending the cycle of abuse. Here is an example of Safety Planning While Living With An Abusive Partner taken from The Domestic Violence Hotline.

• Identify your partner's use and level of force so that you can assess the risk of physical danger to you and your children before it occurs.

• Identify safe areas of the house where there are no weapons and there are ways to escape. If arguments occur, try to move to those areas.

• Don't run to where the children are, as your partner may hurt them as well.

• If violence is unavoidable, make yourself a small target. Dive into a corner and curl up into a ball with your face protected and arms around each side of your head, fingers entwined.

- If possible, have a phone accessible at all times and know what numbers to call for help. Know where the nearest public phone is located. Know the phone number to your local battered women's shelter. If your life is in danger, call the police.

- Let trusted friends and neighbors know of your situation and develop a plan and visual signal for when you need help.

- Teach your children how to get help. Instruct them not to get involved in the violence between you and your partner. Plan a code word to signal to them that they should get help or leave the house.

- Tell your children that violence is never right, even when someone they love is being violent. Tell them that neither you, nor they, are at fault or are the cause of the violence, and that when anyone is being violent, it is important to stay safe.

- Practice how to get out safely. Practice with your children.

- Plan for what you will do if your children tells your partner of your plan or if your partner otherwise finds out about your plan.

- Keep weapons like guns and knives locked away and as inaccessible as possible.

- Make a habit of backing the car into the driveway and keeping it fueled. Keep the driver's door unlocked and others locked — for a quick escape.

- Try not to wear scarves or long jewelry that could be used to strangle you.

- Create several plausible reasons for leaving the house

at different times of the day or night.

Source: The National Domestic Violence Hotline

http://www.thehotline.org/

Help for Survivors

Starting over after surviving domestic violence can be traumatic. You are leaving a familiar life and venturing out to something new. Your relationships and your outlook on life changes. Here are some tips to help ensure that you don't fall back into an abusive relationship.

1.   Surround yourself with support- Spend time with friends and family members who care about you and can support you when you don't feel strong.

2.   Attend a domestic violence support group. It's very therapeutic to learn and share in a supportive setting.

3.   Attend counseling and/or therapy

4.   Practice self care. Indulge in your hobbies and interest. Look for ways to be happy!

5.   Cut off contact with your ex

6.   Be patient with yourself. It takes time to heal from the physical, psychological, financial and emotional wounds that domestic violence makes in your life

7.   Redefine yourself. Don't let domestic violence define you. It might have been part of your story, but it's not who you are.

8.   Give Back- Share your story and insight with others in order to bring awareness of Domestic Violence.

Signs of a Healthy Relationship

After someone experiences Domestic Violence, it is hard to determine what a Healthy Relationship looks like. As part of my healing process, I attended a weekly support group for domestic violence survivors. The one thing that everyone struggled with was knowing when a relationship is healthy. Many survivors said that they didn't trust their own judgment about relationships and didn't have any model of a healthy relationship. Here are a few characteristics of people in a healthy relationship. As you review the list, think about anything that you would like to add.

1.	They allow for individuality

2.	They bring out the best qualities in a partner

3.	They accept endings

4.	They experience openness to change and exploration

5.	They invite growth in the other partner

6.	They experience true intimacy

7.	They feel the freedom to ask honestly for what is wanted

8.	They do not attempt to change or control the other

9.	They encourage self-sufficiency of their partner

10.	They accept commitment

11.	They have a high self esteem

12.	They express feelings spontaneously

13.	They welcome closeness, risk vulnerability

14.	They experience both oneness with and separateness from a partner

Source: San Leandro Community Counseling

Acknowledgements

There are countless people who I want to thank for your support.

Detective Hansen of the Laurel (MD) Police Department, University of Maryland Medical Center (Shock Trauma Center team); Dr. Carnell Cooper, Dr. Thomas Le, Dr. Sajeev Kathuria, Sharon Moore and the ICU Nurses, Domestic Violence Center of Howard County, Camille, Michelle and Diane of Cole Stevens Salon and Day Spa (Greenbelt, MD), Bernard and Monie Broadus, Rev. Bernette Lee Jones, Rev. Eric O. Donaldson, Lavonne Sumler, Bonnie Barnes, my cousin Pam, Carlton Brewington, Deborah Ruffin, Rev. Adara Walton, Donna and Peter Wallace, Dr. Lisa Slade-Martin, Janine Mixon, Shamiere Bridgeford, Amy Washington, Jonathan Fleming, Nikia Austin, Steve Dorsey, Monica and Jerry Montgomery, Margaret and Davis Peyton, Bob Barnes, Darlene Daniels, Harry and Melissa Stuart, Priscilla Giusti, Priscilla Sequria, John Kelley, Lynn Porraro, Sheryl Lane, Angela Taylor, Miracle Wanzo, Michelle Irving, Mika Grace, Veronica Hill, Darrell Jones of Body Mechanix, Predencier Marshall, Alan Holman, Matt Benyo, my neighbor Marsha, Kim Taylor, Linnet Cabin, Martin Smith, Kurt Schake, Michelle Casto, Surina Aguilar, Tisa Peyton, Mary Tate-Smith and Vincent Smith.

Special thanks to my friends and family who have contributed to this book – Jim and Rae Jean Taylor, Dwayne Taylor, Eric Taylor, Tonia Reed, Yvonne (Smith) Jones, Andrea Bullock, Jennie Kinsfather, and Charisse Ewing.